The Shakespeare Handbooks: Shakespeare's Contemporaries
Series Editors: Paul Edmondson & Kevin Ewert

*The Changeling* by Thomas Middleton and William Rowley is a luridly sensual dramatic work which was highly regarded in its day but then largely forgotten until its revival three hundred years later. This timely Handbook:

- offers a detailed theatrical commentary which tracks the motivations of the capricious characters and explores performance possibilities
- examines the cultural conditions that gave rise to the play, juxtaposing them with the conditions of the twentieth century
- analyses early performances as well as later stage and film productions
- presents key critical debates and assessments of *The Changeling*.

**Jay O'Berski** is Assistant Professor of the Practice of Theater Studies at Duke University. He is Artistic Director of the Little Green Pig Theatrical Concern and Associate Artistic Director of Manbites Dog Theater.

**The Shakespeare Handbooks** are student-friendly introductory guides which offer a new approach to understanding the plays of Shakespeare and his contemporaries in performance. The commentary at the heart of each volume explores the play's theatrical potential, providing an experience as close as possible to seeing it in the theatre. Ideal for students and teachers of Literature and Theatre, as well as actors and directors, the overall aim is to help a reader reach an independent and well-informed view of each play by imagining how it might be rehearsed or performed on stage.

THE SHAKESPEARE HANDBOOKS

Series Editors: Paul Edmondson and Kevin Ewert
(Founding Series Editor: John Russell Brown)


PUBLISHED

| | |
|---|---|
| John Russell Brown | *Hamlet* |
| John Russell Brown | *Macbeth* |
| John Russell Brown | *King Lear* |
| David Carnegie | *Julius Caesar* |
| Paul Edmondson | *Twelfth Night* |
| Bridget Escolme | *Antony and Cleopatra* |
| Kevin Ewert | *Henry V* |
| Alison Findlay | *Much Ado about Nothing* |
| Trevor R. Griffiths | *The Tempest* |
| Stuart Hampton-Reeves | *Measure for Measure* |
| Stuart Hampton-Reeves | *Othello* |
| Margaret Jane Kidnie | *The Taming of the Shrew* |
| Ros King | *The Winter's Tale* |
| James N. Loehlin | *Henry IV, Parts I and II* |
| Jeremy Lopez | *Richard II* |
| Edward L. Rocklin | *Romeo and Juliet* |
| Lesley Wade Soule | *As You Like It* |
| Martin White | *A Midsummer Night's Dream* |

SHAKESPEARE'S CONTEMPORARIES

| | |
|---|---|
| Jay O'Berski | Middleton and Rowley: *The Changeling* |
| Stephen Purcell | Webster: *The White Devil* |
| Martin White | Ford: *'Tis Pity She's a Whore* |

Other titles are currently in preparation

The Shakespeare Handbooks:
*Shakespeare's Contemporaries*

# Thomas Middleton and William Rowley
## *The Changeling*

Jay O'Berski

palgrave
macmillan

First published 2012 by
PALGRAVE MACMILLAN

Palgrave Macmillan in the UK is an imprint of Macmillan Publishers Limited, registered in England, company number 785998, of Houndmills, Basingstoke, Hampshire RG21 6XS.

Palgrave Macmillan in the US is a division of St Martin's Press LLC, 175 Fifth Avenue, New York, NY 10010.

Palgrave Macmillan is the global academic imprint of the above companies and has companies and representatives throughout the world.

Palgrave® and Macmillan® are registered trademarks in the United States, the United Kingdom, Europe and other countries.

ISBN-13: 978–0–230–24606–5 hardback
ISBN-13: 978–0–230–24607–2 paperback

This book is printed on paper suitable for recycling and made from fully managed and sustained forest sources. Logging, pulping and manufacturing processes are expected to conform to the environmental regulations of the country of origin.

A catalogue record for this book is available from the British Library.

A catalog record for this book is available from the Library of Congress.

10  9  8  7  6  5  4  3  2  1
21  20  19  18  17  16  15  14  13  12

Printed in China

*For Dana Marks*

# Contents

# Series Editors' Preface

The Shakespeare Handbooks provide an innovative way of studying the plays of Shakespeare and his contemporaries in performance. The commentaries, which are their core feature, enable a reader to envisage the words of a text unfurling in performance, involving actions and meanings not readily perceived except in rehearsal or performance. The aim is to present the plays in the environment for which they were written and to offer an experience as close as possible to an audience's progressive experience of a production.

While each book has the same range of contents, their authors have been encouraged to shape them according to their own critical and scholarly understanding and their first-hand experience of theatre practice. The various chapters are designed to complement the commentaries: the cultural context of each play is presented together with quotations from original sources; the authority of its text or texts is considered with what is known of the earliest performances; key performances and productions of its subsequent stage history are both described and compared; an account is given of influential criticism of the play and the more significant is quoted extensively. The aim in all this has been to help readers to develop their own informed and imaginative view of a play in ways that supplement the provision of standard editions and are more user-friendly than detailed stage histories or collections of criticism from diverse sources.

We would like to acknowledge a special debt of gratitude to the founder of the Shakespeare Handbooks Series, John Russell Brown, whose energy for life, literature and theatre we continue to find truly inspiring.

Paul Edmondson and Kevin Ewert

# *Acknowledgements*

Overwhelming gratitude is due to my friend and editor Kevin Ewert. Thank you for your sage guidance and artistic fervour with this play and many others.

I owe a great debt to the librarians of Lilly Library at Duke University, especially Sara and Danette, but they're all my favourites. And to Lady X for additional research advice.

Thanks to Ellen, Sarah (Jane), Jeffrey and all my colleagues at Duke. And to Little Green Pig and Manbites Dog for constant stimulation.

Randal Robinson, thank you for opening a door into the dangerous parlour of the Jacobeans. I hope to never leave.

# 1 The Text and Early Performances

Jacobean playwrights played well with others. Unlike the un-credited collaboration from which Shakespeare mostly likely benefited, paired teams of writers like Middleton and Rowley, Beaumont and Fletcher, and Barksted and Machin were common in the early seventeenth century. Much like contemporary film or television writers, these men were able to unite on projects where there was a clear distribution of labour. They worked at a fevered pace on a product that wasn't perceived as a revered cultural form so much as ephemeral entertainment constantly required to deliver novelty and excitement to sate its audience. As with Shakespeare's plays these now-classical Jacobean texts were likely written as something more akin to the modern blockbuster than foreseen as enduring treasures. That's doesn't preclude the best (and *The Changeling* is among the very best) from containing deep, probing plots and characters who speak of universal dilemmas while sugaring the pill with plenty of action and eroticism.

Perhaps no Jacobean play features a pair of voices so distinct in content yet unified in theme as *The Changeling*. Thomas Middleton (1580–1627) was a writer by profession, one who did it all. Wildly prolific as a playwright of tragedies, comedies, masques, and pageants, he is believed to have collaborated during his journeyman days with Shakespeare on late plays like the feverishly experimental *Timon of Athens*. Middleton had experienced poverty and like many of his colleagues his vast output as a writer was likely his way of keeping out of debtors' prison. He honed his craft on his early 'city comedies' which were extremely topical and skewered the mores of his time. For his greatest works he was almost exclusively a co-author with playwrights like John Webster and Thomas Dekker but his main collaborator in his last decade as a writer was William Rowley. Together they wrote *A Fair Quarrel*, *The Old Law*, and mostly likely *The Spanish Gypsy*, which features plot points similar to those in *The Changeling*. Unlike the contracted Shakespeare, Middleton was able to work as a free agent for many theatre companies, his style ranging from earthy sex comedies to heady poetic tragedies to the genre-bending, anti-Catholic *A Game at Chess*, the biggest hit of his day. He was such a huge star that it's puzzling why he now comes in such a distant second to Shakespeare in popularity.

William Rowley (1585–1626), unlike Middleton was a wealthy man and foremost an actor. Performing in several companies, most extensively with Prince Charles' Men, Rowley specialized in playing fat-man clown roles and much of his work features parts he may have written with himself in mind. He may have appeared in *The Changeling* as Antonio, Lollio, or Dr. Alibius.

It's largely accepted that Middleton wrote the main 'castle' plot while Rowley handled the 'madhouse' subplot. In order to obsessively equalize the line count, Rowley likely also contributed scenes at the beginning and the end of the play. Critical consensus on a breakdown looks like this:

Middleton: II, III i–ii, IV i, Vi–ii
Rowley: I.i–ii, III iii, IV iii, V iii
IV ii is divided evenly between the two writers

The marvel of the shared responsibilities in writing this play is the number of direct themes and references the two plots have in common. Whether or not experts can discern the stylistic tendencies that make a line Middleton's or Rowley's, the whole feels like the work of one sharp, relentless dramatic mind. The fact that Rowley most likely set up the main plot's introduction and resolution further blurs the lines of 'ownership' of the two plots. Middleton's tragedy is laced with wicked humour and Rowley's comedy is bleakly perilous, unifying the work into an organic whole.

Much will be made in the following chapters arguing the worth of Rowley's subplot since there is some debate as to whether the play works best on stage and in film by retaining only the main tragic plot. The comic plot has fluctuated in and out of vogue since it was first played when Jacobean audiences loved it and made it likely the more popular of the two threads in its day. The role of the sham fool Antonio is billed in the dramatis personae as the eponymous 'changeling' (though one can really take her pick in this play of liars and imposters). Three drolls (short comic sketches) were taken from the play and published in *The Marrow of Complements* in 1655 and an illustration of 'The Changeling' appears beside the likes of Shakespeare's Falstaff on a title page of Francis Kirkman's *The Wits* in 1662 (forty years after *The Changeling* made its debut). Comic stars Timothy Reade, William Robbins, and Thomas Sheppey achieved playing Antonio. So much attention is paid to the characters of Beatrice-Joanna and De Flores in criticism since the early twentieth century that it's difficult to conceive of a time when they were not the roles that most excited the audience's interest.

The madhouse plot was almost universally scorned and dismissed by nineteenth- century critics when the play was only read and not presented on stage. It regained some popularity in the tumultuous 1960s and 1970s but one has a right to be dubious as to whether laughing at the emotionally disturbed will ever come back into vogue after the twentieth century's greater sensitivity towards mental illness and its treatment. More often than not cuts are made to this plot in modern productions, sometimes to the point of eliminating it altogether. A three-hour running time is also a consideration for most theatre companies and the madhouse plot, as in the arcane clown banter scenes in Shakespeare, is often the first to be trimmed.

The main 'castle' plot can now be analysed from a sexual-political standpoint that would have been unimaginable in Jacobean times. The greater ramifications of the thoughts and deeds of the anti-heroes Beatrice and De Flores are now so in tune with pop psychology after Freud that it's difficult to accept what Middleton and Rowley may have meant to be a straightforward morality play about evil undoing good, echoed in Garden of Eden imagery throughout the work.

## Texts

If you were shopping for a compelling read in 1653 London you might try a shop called the Prince's Arms in St Paul's. You would be able to buy a quarto of *The Changeling* by Middleton and Rowley for six pennies – little more than a cheap 'groundling' ticket to a public, outdoor theatre, about the same price as a 'Lord's room' (private box) but less than a ticket to a private indoor theatre.

But you wouldn't be able to see the play on stage. All theatres had been closed down since 1642 due to England's civil wars. During the reactionary Interregnum acting as a profession became illegal and attending theatricals was a crime that could be heavily fined (though intrepid members of the nobility still held private showings). In 1656 the first public showings began to creep back into the open, though the word 'play' was avoided under the Protectorate of Oliver Cromwell, the de facto king. You'd have to wait until 1657 to see *The Changeling* at the reopened Phoenix, but by 1660 audiences were moving on to the more salacious (but decidedly less violent) excesses of the Restoration under noted libertine Charles II.

Rights to the play may have been sold to Humphrey Moseley to help pay the overwhelming debts of theatrical manager William Beeston, who had submitted it to the King for protection in 1639. There is speculation that Beeston may have commissioned Middleton and Rowley to write a pot-boiler that became *The Changeling* based on sources that were fresh off the presses. Beeston ran the Cockpit theatre until he lost it and went to debtors' prison. Luckily, Moseley was able to keep plays like *The Changeling* (including some by Shakespeare) alive and in circulation during the eighteen years of 'dark nights' for the London stage.

Registered in 1652, *The Changeling* was listed as a comedy and attributed only to Rowley. The quarto edition of the play featuring both authors' names was published in 1653 by bookseller Thomas Newcomb. No company of players is credited, simply that it 'was Acted (with great Applause) at the Privat house in Drury-Lane, and Salisbury Court'. When Moseley died in 1661 his daughter Anne took over the business. When a second quarto of the play came out in 1668, a new title page featured Anne's initials and credited the Duke of York's company of actors. Nine copies of the original sheets of this issue escaped the Great Fire of 1666, perhaps in the crypt of St Paul's. The quarto edition's late date of publication, twenty plus years after the first performance of *The Changeling* is unusual and suggests that the playwrights, who died in 1627 (Middleton) and 1625 or 1626 (Rowley), had little to say about the printed version. This is not surprising when one considers how many plays, credited and un-credited, both men wrote; especially Middleton who now seems the likely author of *The*

*Revenger's Tragedy*, a play that appeared anonymously and for centuries was attributed to Cyril Tourneur. It was a time when playwrights had to be prolific to make any money and willing to release all claims to acting companies, the de facto owners of any scripts they produced.

Where exactly the copy of the play that ended up in Moseley's hands came from is a matter of conjecture. N.W. Bawcutt at first suggested that it was mostly likely a prompt-script due to the practical stage directions and lack of uniform spelling typical to authorial foul papers. He later let go of this claim but evidence of possibly cut scenes like the much-anticipated dance of the madhouse inmates could substantiate that the quarto was directly adapted from a prompt book rather than from the writers' foul papers. While Michael Neill posits that the 'missing' morris dance may have been performed as a bergomask dance after the written epilogue, Gary Taylor is satisfied that the stage direction *"The Madmen and Fools Dance [to music]"* in Act V scene 3 wraps up the madhouse wedding preparations neatly. Taylor is most comfortable with the quarto originating from a prompt-copy while Gary Walton Williams finds traction in the theory that a 'fair scribal transcript' from foul papers accounts for the many mistakes in the text.

Despite the play's great popularity on stage at the time, the two issues of the quarto in the mid-seventeenth century were the last times it appeared in print until 1815. This gaping hole in the life of *The Changeling* is part of the enigma of how a great play can effectively disappear for centuries.

## First performances

First licensed by Sir Henry Herbert, Master of Revels, on 7 May 1622, for Lady Elizabeth's Servants at the Phoenix, *The Changeling* was selected for a court performance in January of 1624. A splinter company, the Queen of Bohemia's, took the play to the Salisbury Court that year. It enjoyed a long run at the Phoenix, with occasional breaks due to plague, remaining in repertory until 1636 (Queen Henrietta's Company took it over after Elizabeth's Men disbanded in 1625). Interrupted from further production by the civil wars beginning in 1642, *The Changeling* was revived at Salisbury Court again in 1659 by the Duke of York's Company. On 23 February diarist

Samuel Pepys, having seen the play in Whitefriars, remarked that 'it takes exceedingly'. The play stayed in repertory at the Duke of York's Theatre until at least 1661. It was revived in the same venue in 1668 and although it appeared in adapted form as William Hayley's watered-down melodrama *Marcella* in 1789, *The Changeling* would have to wait just under three centuries to become in vogue again.

The plays of the Restoration, while ribald and clever, avoid the sense of Grand Guignol darkness that distinguish the Jacobeans. One would have to wait for two World Wars to ravage Europe before the erotic psychology and black irony of a play like *The Changeling* would again catch fire on professional stages (though some of these plays were staged in the first half of the 20th century on amateur ones). While some posit that this nearly 300-year gap in performance was due to the lack of a romantic sensibility in the play, others feel the characters and psychology of *The Changeling* were ahead of their time. While a few Jacobean plays like John Webster's *The Duchess of Malfi* experienced a revival of interest in the nineteenth century, many more like Middleton's *The Revenger's Tragedy* and John Ford's *'Tis Pity She's a Whore* suffered a gap in production similar to *The Changeling*. Whatever the cause for the extended hiatus, the play found a new audience during the turmoil of the 1960s and 1970s and has remained a much-studied classic ever since. That few professional productions of the play are attempted may be more a testament to the large cast size and the darkness of its themes in a twenty-first century market that favours small casts, lightweight comedies, and spectacle-driven musicals.

# 2  *Commentary: the Play in Performance*

## Introduction

There are numberless ways to analyse a play but I'll be focusing on a practical, page-to-stage method that comes out of contemporary actor/director training. In the late nineteenth and early twentieth centuries Konstantin Stanislavsky became the progenitor of a structured way of thinking about making plays. Although he never formalized any strict method (contrary to many people's confusion with the Americanized 'Method' he unwittingly inspired), Stanislavsky did, by the end of his long life in art, boil down almost everything the actor does to *action*. Acting is action shown on a stage and the actor's role is to divine what intentions the character must pursue based on clues inherent in the text. Stanislavsky freely admitted his ideas were superfluous in analysing how to play Shakespeare because there was no subtext, unlike with psychological fare like Chekhov, Ibsen or almost any contemporary play we make today. In Shakespeare nine times out of ten if one character tells another, 'I smite thee!' it means duck. We know what a character is thinking because she says it aloud, whether publicly or privately in an aside.

But what about the later Jacobeans? In a play like *The Changeling* it often seems like 'no' means 'yes' means 'maybe'. With an opaque character like Beatrice-Johanna, intentions can no longer always be taken at face value. Her progression or 'arc' from a conflicted virgin in love with Alsemero to the conspiring lover of her nemesis De Flores is a deeply nuanced journey that has challenged many of the greatest actors of our times.

This is a play where characters are driven by their darkest desires, passions that we don't talk about in public. To realize *The Changeling* in a truthful way it's especially important for the actor to be aware of what's really going on in the psyche of their role and to take it one step at a time without skipping any moments. A common truism in theatre is that an actor needs to 'turn his back' on events that will happen later in the play. In other words 'don't play the ending'. Surprise us. While it's important to blindside the audience with exciting revelations and twists, the actor works out a 'road map' in and out of rehearsals where she can chart the course of how a role will play out on stage. It's this hyper-awareness of human nature at work in a role and the ability to seamlessly reveal the character's journey that makes us believe a great actor simply *is* the part he plays.

I'll be using a practical actor/director's approach to break the text into bite-sized *beats*. A beat is a stage term for a section of text that can be identified as having a clear beginning and an end. This unit of dramatic action can be scrutinized on its own so one can analyse it closely rather than losing specific moments in the expanse of the big picture. A beat can't be empirically chosen (i.e. there is no one way to select where they fall) but for our purposes I'll be breaking up the text based on crucial *events* and the characters' reactions to them. An event is an occurrence that affects the majority of characters on stage, changing what they *desire* from one another, even if only fractionally. The most obvious events are ones where a new character enters or an onstage character exits, but they also include physical events (like a vase breaking or a bomb exploding) or revelations (someone saying 'I love you' or 'I'm not really your father'). For the actor, identification of an event and just how it changes what her character desires is a strong way to plot shifts and levels in the life of the role. The director's job is to encourage and edit these switches, seeing the bigger picture and making sure it all adds up to tell as clear a story as possible.

*The Changeling* is so full of twists and reversals that it's particularly ripe for what is known as *action analysis*, the identification of what's driving the characters to do what they do. This is a technique favoured by directors and actors based on the writings of Stanislavsky and many contemporary directors in the West call it by similar names. Max Stafford-Clark's 'actioning' is an example of this process, one within which directors and actors can speak to each other in objective, action-based terms rather than vague emotional or quality-based ones (e.g. 'Hamlet should be angrier', 'Ophelia is sexy here'). Not only does this way of working bring light to an intricate text, it respects the sensitivities of the artists involved. The more concrete and impersonal the foundational structure can be, the more the extremely intimate and exposed work of any artist can be supported with tact and care.

While great actors bring a wealth of ideas to the table to be sculpted by the director, the latter also offers imagery and ways of attacking a scene. The ideal is to avoid the dictatorial (unless perhaps one is staging a spectacle based on a singular vision) and to collaborate in an effort to *tell the truth*. In the commentary below I'll offer options of how a scene or role might be approached. Thankfully there is no one way to play *The Changeling* and therein lies the challenge and excitement of reading and creating a work of art.

Note: all references are taken from the New Mermaids 2006 edition.

# Act I

### Act I, scene i

**1–12** The Jacobeans did not employ sets and props the way modern productions do. Many plays from this period begin with a lone narrator acting as chorus or a conversation that similarly sets up exposition that introduces a problem to the audience. In *The Changeling* our chorus is Alsemero who, alone at the top, could be standing anywhere or nowhere. Unlike most modern plays, there are very few stage directions in Jacobean scripts, so modern directors and designers must make a choice about just what the performer should be doing physically and what environment in which to place the actor. In the case of Alsemero he may either be talking to the audience or to himself. If it's to the audience, who do *they* represent but *himself*? The conventions of the aside and the soliloquy demand that lines are often crossed between speaking to other characters and talking to the audience. The first twelve lines of the play are *private thoughts* and set the tone for the battle between what's out in the open and what's hidden away in secrecy. It's no coincidence that these opening lines are spoken by a man trying to convince himself it's okay to pursue a beautiful stranger he just met in church. His partner and sounding board in the scene is *us*, the audience. This makes us an active participant in Alsemero's decision to stay in Alicante and pursue Beatrice. We become invested in the two would-be lovers getting together and at this point we see no obstacle in Alsemero's way that should keep him from seeing more of this 'perfection'.

As far as choice of location, Alsemero could still be in the church where for the second time he's seen Beatrice. This might be the most visually striking image, especially if the service is in progress, since the audience can hear Alsemero's romantic thoughts while Beatrice is spotlighted and identified as his beloved. A sudden change of location would be required, however, when Jasperino arrives, unless the characters can somehow whisper through the service. This seems unlikely and a new location is eventually required so Alsemero could begin just outside the church, a location suggested by post-service bell tolling. Or he could be on the wharf, hoping to convince himself to leave this tempting woman behind and embark on a naval adventure. Modern productions are often more akin to Jacobean ones in that a fluid stagecraft dictates shifting locations, most often indicated by lighting (while Jacobeans relied on the words to set the scene and mood). Perhaps Alsemero remembers the church and we hear the bells and see the colours of the stained glass but he's not actually 'inside' it, revealed as the lights and sound change it to a street or wharf. The days of large, spectacular sets for non-musicals are currently over so directors of straight plays most often rely on 'impressionistic' staging to tell a multi-location story.

Turning to the content of Alsemero's soliloquy, the play begins with an omen, a tingling warning that mistakes will be made. This red flag is raised at the introduction to a love-at-first-sight story that, much like Shakespeare's *Romeo and Juliet*, is a cautionary tale against rash decisions and letting Eros rule over Reason. As with all great thrillers, our unsuspecting victim shakes off his sense of dread and marches into the haunted house. Although quickly dismissed, a momentary dark tone here will get the ball rolling for a tension that escalates throughout the play.

Images of temples and churches abound as the characters' strain to rationalize their holy versus profane actions. Alsemero convinces himself that pursuing Beatrice is a blessed endeavour because he first saw her in a church. Note how God and the Church are not called on for strength or guidance after this first speech.

This first speech also sets up the idea of the 'eye of the beholder'. Alsemero introduces Beatrice to us as a holy vision. Even before we see her we are set up to adore her since we've been told she's beautiful and perfect. This kind of propaganda goes a long way to blind us to the real Beatrice we'll get to know soon. It's true that audiences tend to believe what they're told, an important tool in 'misdirecting' them so they can experience the thrill and terror of later reversals. 'Man's first creation' refers to the Garden of Eden – a good starting place for a story that ends in the darkness of Hell. Alsemero sets himself up for a Fall to rival Adam's by placing his faith in an unreliable 'Eve' (which later makes De Flores the Serpent, as he is so often described). He rationalizes that he can return Adam to his 'right home back' (i.e. pre-Fall Paradise) if he succeeds in winning Beatrice. 'So there's beginning and perfection too' is apropos since the playwrights have set up three major themes and a harbinger of doom in just twelve lines. Romeo's first sight of Juliet is an earlier relative of this scene and perhaps a template for playing it.

**13–53**   In a scene perhaps borrowed from Shakespeare's *The Merchant of Venice*, Jasperino's motivation is to get his friend Alsemero on a ship. Alsemero baulks at his advice, having 'observed the temple's vane to turn full in my face' and summoning up his holy mandate to be with Beatrice. Alsemero's motivation is to convince Jasperino that he (Alsemero) should stay. The two desires run counter to one another, so the characters/actors can push against one another to create conflict.

As in *Merchant of Venice*, Jasperino asks if Alsemero is feeling quite himself, describing him as a man prone to rash decisions and stubborn fortitude in executing them. Of course Jasperino is unintentionally right on the mark about Alsemero's latest intended 'voyage' and even mentions 'orisons' (prayers) to evoke Alsemero's 'church' and 'devotion' images. Jasperino is in the dark as to Alsemero's motive: his burning desire for Beatrice. Evidently his friend is not exactly a ladies' man even though his friends and mother have been trying to set him up for ages. A common method for an actor's 'building' a role is to take everything that's said about the character by other characters and using that composite as a framework on which to build up mannerisms and intentions. If we start with Jasperino's description of his friend then one assumes Alsemero is a man too busy with travelling to fall in love. Using this characteristic as the 'seed' an actor builds from, impetuosity becomes the key to the role. If Alsemero is first introduced as a look-before-you-leap character then that's a facet that can continually inform every other decision made by the actor in how to play the role.

Another unwitting harbinger occurs in the use of the image of 'violence' that has a double meaning here. How much these pointers should be played up is the choice of the actor and director. Should the audience feel a sense of unease already or be misdirected into a sense of romantic anticipation for the approaching affair? Even more than Jasperino, Servant 2 presages bad events in his 'We must not to sea today, this smoke will bring forth fire'. Set up as an aside by an early editor (and therefore open to our modern interpretation), it could instead be directed to Servant 1. If addressed directly to the audience a self-aware 'Hang onto your hats, folks!' connection can be established. De Flores continues this practice throughout the play so why not set it up here? When Alsemero describes his business on land to the servants as an 'affair', a modern audience could easily take this to elude to an 'affair of the heart', although the term wasn't in use during the Jacobean period.

For a possible physical action here the two friends could be moving a trunk filled with Alsemero's possessions. If Jasperino is intent on getting the object into the ship and Alsemero is unhelpful, even reversing the direction of the trunk, then an image is created of two men working at cross purposes. This would also substantiate the introduction of the servants to finish the arrested job of packing for a journey. Any physical action that assists the storytelling by compelling the actors to show rather than purely tell is a visual asset and raises the stakes for the actors. The lack of stage directions in Jacobean plays allows the actors and the director to make choices that are often explicitly proscribed in modern play scripts.

**54–8**  Beatrice enters with her waiting woman, Diaphanta, and other servants, and while there is no stage direction indicating where she comes from we can infer that it's the church. What we don't know is where she's going, so an important choice needs to be made here. Has she come to boldly and romantically confront Alsemero? It seems unlikely since for the moment she's sitting on information about her current marital status. Beatrice could be emerging from the church and unwittingly stumble on the men in conversation. This makes her seem less complicit romantically than actively looking for her admirer. Or she might be rashly confronting the man who has been staring intently at her in church for the last two Sundays. Another choice is that she could have sought out the visiting sailor Alsemero down at the wharf while making it look like she's just out on a stroll with her entourage. This choice is the most active for Beatrice, giving her the most agency (though perhaps casting her as a manipulator from the start). Editors insert a bow and a kiss by Alsemero (suggested by Jasperino's lines) but exactly what kind of action occurs here is chosen by the actor and director. Obviously a formal 'pleased to meet you' kiss is less threatening than a 'let's run away together!' one. A hint is that Jasperino is shocked by what he sees, either meaning Alsemero has been a coldly chaste 'stoic' (so even a formal kiss would be shocking) or that the heat is truly on in their steamy greeting. What kind of a kiss here also sets the tone for Beatrice's persona. There's a world of difference between a kiss on the hand, cheek or lips, especially between strangers. Our first impressions of Beatrice are immediately set up before she ever speaks.

**59–75** There ensues a lovers' *pas de deux* in words that has its own strong warnings built in. The battle between judgement and 'rash' desire is set up here with Beatrice championing the former. She warns him to double check the signals his eyes are sending him since they might be blind. Alsemero blithely pushes her warning aside, a victim of love (or lust?) at first sight. How hard is she lobbying for him to desist? She's obviously tempted by Alsemero but is this a case of true love or just the way she operates? If the actor playing Beatrice decides that she is indeed in love with Alsemero then it raises the stakes for her to do whatever is necessary to be with him. If that were the case she might be making a weak argument here for Alsemero to question falling in love with her at first sight. Pure lust, while a strong motivator, might set her up as character that cries wolf and is capable of falling for every new man who comes along.

The mating dance between Beatrice and Alsemero is a brief one so their body language must be as clear as possible here. Just how virginal and naive should Beatrice appear in her proximity to her suitor? Anything conspiratorial and sensual in this exchange could easily set Beatrice up as either a conniving villainess or a modern woman living without fear of social repercussions for her boldness. While both are examples of strong playing, these choices actually lower the stakes for the character. The strongest choice here would involve making the audience an active participant in 'solving' the riddle of whether or not the two should get together. A lack of subtlety from either actor could tip the scales too far into the negative. The audience would be relegated to passively waiting for bad things to happen to this rash pair of strangers.

**76–87**    The event here is Alsemero's very hasty proposal of marriage in which he claims he lacks only Beatrice's consent. What might have been a subtle flirtation is taken to the next level by the seriousness of his offer. Beatrice's 'Oh, there's one above me, sir' has a surface meaning in that her father actually controls her destiny but there's subtext there which will be later revealed. Her frustration here will express just how trapped versus empowered she feels as she either despairs or begins to scheme how to get out of the mess we don't yet know she's in.

Jasperino employs a ship-as-sex image in his decision to ape his friend, Alsemero. This clown character speaks in prose while the lovers speak in blank verse or iambic pentameter. This signals his comic potential as in Shakespeare's characters like Mercutio and Falstaff. Although he is a friend of Alsemero, prose may also signal that he's rough-around-the-edges (perhaps even lower in class) than the poetry-speaking Alsemero. Jasperino makes a distinction in seeking a 'lawful prize' to 'board', foreshadowing the unwitting Alsemero's rude awakenings to come. The latter assumes he's the only suitor with a stake in the game.

**88–102**    De Flores enters on the heels of Jasperino's pirate image and becomes part of a dual 'wooing' scene. While Jasperino and Diaphanta flirt and get bawdy *soto voce* (they have no stage direction to actually leave the stage) the awkward exchange between Beatrice and De Flores stands in vivid counterpoint to the clowns' low-stakes fun. Although in line with Shakespeare's great antagonist-protagonists Richard III, Macbeth and Iago, De Flores most closely resembles Aaron the Moor from *Titus Andronicus* in his humble lack of status and his willingness to go to any ends to get what he wants. The question is whether to make him first appear as a wolf in sheep's clothing or as a figure of dread. His very first line is curtly interrupted by Beatrice and we immediately see a relationship encumbered by acrimonious baggage. Is De Flores merely delivering an innocuous message or is he actively breaking up her courtship? As with all choices made on stage there are more passive and more active options. If De Flores consciously acts to get closer to Beatrice and remove any obstacles to that proximity, these are active and exciting motivations for the actor, however subtle he plays them.

Announcing the impending arrival of her father, De Flores is immediately ignored and left to his own analysis of Beatrice's hatred of him. In what is clearly an aside to the audience he's willing, for now, to bide his time and whet his appetite for Beatrice with his eyes. Is this the peeping of a lustful stalker or an unrequited lover? Does he live in hope of proving himself worthy of her or is he just looking for an opportunity to ravish her when she's off balance? As with all soliloquies, there is an argument made here. The audience is entreated to join in, preferably on the side of the speaker. It's the beginning of our relationship with De Flores and he asks us to tell him he's right to keep trying to make Beatrice notice and be kind to him. We are actually his scene partner here and the actor discerns a motivation as clearly when playing with the audience as he does when acting with another actor.

**103–131** De Flores' interruption drives the flirting couple closer together and Beatrice's motivation is to get Alsemero on her side against him. The flow of the tryst between the lovers is poisoned by the intrusion of the 'basilisk', a monster so hideous it turns its victims into stone. This opens the debate as to just how ugly De Flores really is. Directors and actors have wrestled with just how much his disfigurement is in the eye of the beholder. Does Beatrice see him as monstrous simply because of her antipathy (or attraction) to him? Is the plot served or sabotaged by a traditionally unattractive De Flores? What is 'ugly' when represented on stage and will it register equally to all audience members? Middleton and Rowley do not tell us that this servant has a hare lip, burns, or birthmarks and so the actor/director/designer make a judgement call much as they would with the extent of the deformities exhibited in a portrayal of Shakespeare's Richard III. A tough call since you're playing with the audience's psyche here. Little or no ugliness and the audience may think 'What's her problem?' Employ grotesque make-up and suspension of disbelief may be an issue (not to mention a danger of 'camp' if the effects are poorly rendered). And yet danger is the spice of life in drama so something *must* be ventured to be gained. A 'hideous' De Flores might start to grow on the audience and he might begin to look like the 'normal' one as the play progresses (like John Merrick in *The Elephant Man*).

Alsemero's motivation may be to calm the flustered Beatrice by justifying and normalizing her hatred of De Flores. His 'There's scarce a thing but is both loved and loathed' either gets to the root of the love–hate duality Beatrice wrestles with or it simply means 'different strokes for different folks'. Alsemero exposes his own irrational distaste for cherries, which raises a contextual question. Although the double entendre of 'cherry' for 'virginity' does not seem to have come into use until the twentieth century, a modern audience will almost assuredly hear the salacious meaning in Alsemero's reply. Whether he plays up the sexuality inherent in the fruit here could colour the audience's perception of Alsemero as a prince or a rogue. His awkwardness could be his charm or it could be a red flag signalling his capriciousness.

Here we learn that De Flores is respected by her father Vermandero, the keeper of the castle of his daughter's virginity. This raises the stakes for Beatrice in that he's not some easily dismissed messenger that she can remove as an obstacle. The fact raises his status, protecting him from her power in the household.

**132–145**   The naughty dialogue is now audible between Jasperino and Diaphanta. We can assume that Jasperino has been divining whether Beatrice's waiting woman is a 'lawful prize' throughout the scene above and their conversation comes into focus as Alsemero and Beatrice's negotiation continues, fading into the background. The original choice on a Jacobean stage may have been to use the 'inner below' where characters often tarried or hid, implying that they could not be seen by the characters on the main stage. If this scene's location is 'outside the church' the conversation that's not in focus could cross upstage to the steps or side of the building. If the scene takes place on the wharf the duo could sit in a rowboat or on the dock facing up stage.

If Diaphanta and Jasperino have been in conversation for the past forty lines or so, they've had some time to break the ice and speak in erotic riddles. In their discourse the insane asylum subplot is subtly set up and love as a form of madness is broached. There's also a nod to the soporific symptom of Alsemero's alchemical pregnancy test.

Graphic sexual entendres abound in this short exchange in prose and as always with archaic comic references in plays like *The Changeling* the director and actors must decide how much of the content to spell out visually when words fail to impart meaning. 'Cuckoo-what-you-call't' has a great ring to it but to impart its phallic shape and purgative qualities might require a certain amount of mime.

**146–154**  We are introduced to Vermandero, in whose home (castle) this tangled foreground plot takes place. He makes an unwitting slip in his 'your devotion's ended?' while addressing his daughter. Beatrice makes her first bold scheming manoeuvre by making it look like Alsemero desires to see Vermandero's castle (and gain Beatrice's virginity). Her quick-thinking is apparent here, contrasted with the blindsided Vermandero. Alsemero may acknowledge with a look to the audience how impressive this woman's powers of persuasion can be.

**155–179**  Vermandero alludes to the secrets he's hidden away in his stronghold and this sets up the first of the play's two 'farmer's daughter' story lines: the ancient story of the farmer (or any unwitting paternal figure) who lets the young virile lad 'sleep in his hayloft' while nursing an ulterior motive for the farmer's nubile daughter. Alsemero gets a lucky break in that Vermandero knew and admired the young man's father. This is good enough to get him in the castle door, removing the first obstacle to Alsemero's (and Beatrice's) motivation.

This leads into a curious little sidebar where we learn that Alsemero's father, John de Alsemero, perished in the battle between the Spanish and the rebelling Dutch at Gibraltar in 1607. The Treaty of the Hague in 1609 frustrated his son's plans to avenge him. Is this just small talk or a cogent detail? There is almost no 'gristle' in this play that does not directly or symbolically support the actions on the characters; unlike in many of Shakespeare's plays, in this main plot there are few long speeches or random-seeming scenes that can be cut without loss of depth or underlining of key images and themes. So, this could be a harbinger of Alsemero's vengefulness and frustration, and a passionate outburst here might better prepare the audience for his later character flaws. The actor playing him might take it as a cue to flare up violently only to stifle himself quickly, returning to being the perfect mild-mannered house guest.

**180–192**   The bombshell that Beatrice has been hiding drops. This major event is Vermandero's revelation that there's another suitor, in fact a fiancé, involved with his daughter. This roadblock temporarily derails Alsemero's intention of wooing Beatrice and he's looking for a way to exit with what's left of his pride. Vermandero continues the castle theme in describing the groom-to-be, Alonzo de Piracquo, as 'hot preparing for his day of triumph' as if the taking of Beatrice (and her virginity) were the same as storming the castle's gates. A double meaning flows as Beatrice entreats Vermandero not to be so 'violent' in separating her from the 'dear companion of my soul, Virginity' – also meaning, she doesn't want to lose her new lover, Alsemero. Her motivation is to get her father to postpone the wedding. Beatrice might be physically signalling Alsemero that all is well despite the assailable hurdle of her previous engagement. She has another trick or two up her sleeve.

**193–217**   Double meanings abound as Vermandero extends an invitation for Alsemero to stay to see his castle, and for 'her best entertainment' (with an unwitting meaning of sensual high jinks). A spicy Beatrice might play up her father's entendres as the line between his castle and his daughter grows ever thinner. Vermandero would have Alsemero at his daughter's wedding; the new-met lovers obviously wish it was one for them, excluding the current groom. Alsemero's discomfort should be palpable as Vermandero praises his soon-to-be son-in-law. The father is blissfully unaware that there is any subterfuge in the works and his proud boasting should stand in counterpoint to the worried lovers. When Alsemero says it's as if he were being menaced by shot from the 'murderers' (small cannon) at Vermandero's castle gates it creates a difficult image. The problem is to make an audience glean the meaning of an archaic technical term. One suggestion would be to change the word in performance to 'small cannon' for clarity's sake. An explosion sound effect from Alsemero might work (but that could just sound like *gun-toting* murderers) or the line could be cut altogether. The worst effect would be the audience's confusion in thinking that Vermandero employs actual murderers to ward off unsanctioned suitors.

**218–230**   A lover's signal from Beatrice goes all wrong as she drops a glove for Alsemero only to have the 'serpent' De Flores retrieve it. Perhaps she protests too much in casting off the other to join the tainted one with the command to 'draw thy own skin off with 'em!' This edition gives the actor an evocative stage direction in '*Tries to pull the glove onto his hand*'based on De Flores line about how he should 'thrust my fingers into her sockets here'. This might be luridly executed and leave the audience to imagine the sordid use De Flores puts this intimate apparel to when he's behind closed doors. In seeking to 'haunt' Beatrice, De Flores echoes her father in that he'll have his 'will', meaning both his way and the sating of his lust. Classic sex-as-control or frustrated true love? Is there any difference for this man? We've seen De Flores lurking on the periphery and perhaps thought he'd be employed as a go-between for the young lovers, but now the tone darkens with the revelation of his obsession for her. The scene may have begun with a soliloquy by Alsemero but it ends with one by an antagonist who eclipses the 'hero' with his dreadful charisma. There is potential for De Flores to become the one we're cheering for as his cause becomes the more active one and requires the audience's 'consent', even if we know it's a terrible idea. Misdirection at the beginning of the play has us in Alsemero's corner but there's a turning point here where De Flores' dark passion outweighs Alsemero's well-intentioned one.

## Act I, scene ii

**1–38**   The play transitions into William Rowley's secondary plot set in an insane asylum run by an old doctor named Alibius and his trickster assistant, Lollio. On the Jacobean stage no change of settings (or even lighting) slowed down the action. Descriptions of location were *within* the lines themselves and actors had to verbally (and perhaps physically) evoke the atmosphere. For modern productions, much weight is given to the scale and sensation of scenic and lighting design and for a large budget production it would not be a problem to switch often between grand castle and sordid madhouse settings. For a smaller-scale version more invention would be required. Perhaps an area or areas of the stage could permanently represent exclusively the castle vs. the madhouse. Or one set could symbolize both. Or one could follow the Jacobeans and have no set aside from a few movable furniture pieces. Lighting could do the lion's share of the work to create the atmosphere of two locations, perhaps even playing up the synchronicity of theme at the same time. This fluidity of space could play up the juxtaposed ideas that drive both of the parallel storylines. The secret lovers in the first scene are comically mirrored in the madhouse plot. Alibius, like Vermandero, takes Lollio into confidence and trusts him to protect his hot young wife, Isabella, from sexual predation. Lollio offers to 'handle' the sweet, deep 'knowledge' that Alibius puts in his care. As with Vermandero, this old man also seeks to guard the secret of his version of a castle (or rather a cage).

While entrusting Lollio to watch over his wife, the jealous doctor leaves the chicken in the jaws of the fox. Lollio is hardly discreet in his repartee with Alibius. The exchange is pure Groucho Marx, though with plenty of pornographic imagery to stir the groundlings: 'I would wear my ring on my own finger' (Alibius) and 'if it but lie by, one or other will be thrusting into't' (Lollio, echoing De Flores in the previous scene) being bawdy gems. A Jacobean audience would have been more attuned to the subtleties of this wordplay. How much of this should be mimed for a modern, visually oriented audience? The sensibility here for a modern audience most closely resembles vaudeville where often the comic duo stands stiffly side-by-side and rat-a-tats the jokes directly to the audience. Clarity might be lost if the actors were physically active (e.g. Lollio doing physical chores in the asylum while Alibius counts up the ill-gotten gains) but it also might be more engaging to watch than two clowns firing off one liners. Perhaps a combination of the two styles would be most effective.

When Alibius makes the unwitting mistake of telling his warden 'in my absence supply my place' the game is officially afoot. It surely demands some kind of 'take' to the audience by Lollio on 'I'll do my best', whether slyly or with a deadpan poker face.

**39–65**  Lollio distinguishes between the two types of inmates in this asylum: madmen and fools. He might employ an onstage image, like a chalk board, to illustrate how to distinguish the two, or he might shout into the opposing wings and be answered by each opposing 'camp'. Because the text keeps coming back to this distinction an aid could help the audience stick with the theme and tell the difference between Franciscus and Antonio. Alibius qualifies his fears by foolishly disqualifying the inmates from sensual wrong-doing since they are being rehabilitated in his care. Visitors, however, are to be watched like a hawk and kept away from the quarantined Isabella. This mirrors Vermandero's trust of his 'insider' De Flores while fearing attack from outside suitors. In a production of this play it might be a useful move to physically repeat gestures between mirrored characters and use the same areas of the stage wherever mirror moments occur. This could allow the audience to see clearly just why they're being asked to spend time in the loony bin. If they feel like it's just an inter-cutting of simple comic skits the wholeness of Middleton and Rowley's plan is lost. The ideal would be if they can see that the same story can be shown as tragedy or farce. Often critics seem to miss this connection (and damn the subplot as distracting) so playing it up clearly and boldly is advisable.

Lollio begins an ongoing theme that a fool (Lollio) and madman (Alibius) are running the asylum, so surely any visitors are there only to see them and not Isabella (evidently the only sane one). One might ask whether the doctor is simply foolish or truly mad to think Lollio is a reliable gatekeeper for his wife's honour. Requisite to this farmer's daughter chestnut, Alibius completely trusts his over-sexed warden.

**66–78**  Lollio names the hours of the day after parts of body, notably calling the present time 'belly hour', surely because 'rubbing bellies' is on his lurid mind. A sharp physical comedian can elevate this from doggerel to a deft bit of clowning. Or it might be a routine worthy of cutting in a production that aspires to be less than three hours.

**79–91**  Enter Antonio, the character curiously labelled by Middleton and Rowley as 'The Changeling', with his friend, Pedro (contrast this with John Webster's tight lips as to who is actually the title role in his *The White Devil*). Without stage direction it becomes clear that Antonio is dressed in madcap attire and we have Kirkman's frontispiece to *The Wits* to perhaps give us a view of an early costume for Antonio. In this illustration Antonio wears a pointy dunce cap and long gown, and carries a child's primer. Whatever he's wearing, a sight gag is prepared by Alibius' immediate identification of Antonio as his noon 'idiot' appointment. Pedro might even be holding a number like he's waiting to renew his driver's licence or buy meat. This madhouse is such an obvious racket for making money that it's up to the director and designers to take their imagery as far as serves the production. In paying for Antonio's stay, his friend Pedro in essence greases the palm of Isabella's unwitting pimps, her husband and his loyal 'officer'. There may also be reflection here in the marriage industry that Beatrice, her father, and her suitors are a part of.

**92–110** There's evidence that the nickname 'Tony' had its first use here in what became a popular synonym for a fool. Antonio's laughter is a good sign to Lollio that he is not an animal (good to hear that the 'fool' Lollio knows his Aristotle, specifically *De Partibus Animalum III*). Sometimes Antonio is played as mentally retarded; there are a few clues as to just what the physical form of his faux disability should take, for example Lollio's 'Hold up your head'. As with De Flores' deformity the choice is to be made by the artists in the production as to how far Antonio goes to disguise his aristocratic, 'sane' self.

Just as De Flores claims noble birth, his fellow cuckhold-maker, Antonio, is praised by Pedro as a gentleman from 'a great family'. Both men are fallen 'changelings' and the playwright's identification of Antonio as the main shape-shifter may just be a cheeky smokescreen to cloak the more dangerous De Flores. Middleton and Rowley share storylines here, portraying two wolves in sheep's clothing, one a humble servant, one a pitiful 'madman', both aiming to corrupt another man's wife. What are Antonio's motives? Is pure lust enough for the actor to play or does a richer back-story need to be fabricated in absence of textual support?

**111–133** It seems clear that Lollio understands the set-up by this point, 'he looks no other yet' perhaps accompanied by a take to the audience. Lollio plans to oblige the fox with the hen as long as the guard dog gets his due. While offering to raise Antonio to 'the wit of constable' (a low bar to set since constables were typically stooges in contemporary plays), Lollio also hints at the potential to raise the changeling to his (Lollio's) level. Here we have more comparison (and blurring the lines) between the keeper and the inmate, the wise one and the fool. 'I'll be as arrant a fool as he, or he should be as wise as I' is a winking signal to Pedro that everyone's on the same page with this little ruse.

**134–168**  As Pedro exits Antonio lays it on thick with a childish fool routine, and his physical actions might remind us of a kinder-gartener on his first parting from his mother. Lollio, alternately like a heartless captor and a kindly schoolteacher, calms him down with a series of test questions. Antonio answers as the classic zanies do by out-fooling the truly foolish one (as with the Fool in *King Lear*, Feste in *Twelfth Night*, Touchstone in *As You Like It*). When asked 'how many knaves make an honest man' Antonio cannot answer and Lollio explains that the only honest men are reformed criminals (knaves being the brutal justice system). There may be a veiled threat here to warn Antonio that he should check himself where Lollio is in charge, especially if he's going to get to play at 'push-pin', a children's game with obvious sexual connotations.

**169–185**  The ongoing 'Who Is a Fool or a Knave?' question is addressed in the form of a mathematical 'story problem'. Alibius can't follow it (or much else) but Lollio uses visual aids to illustrate, and might best use the two fools (Lollio and Antonio) and one knave (Alibius) at hand. This could be an antic vaudeville routine that morphs into a follow-the-leader or hat-passing gag. 'We three' refers to a popular illustration of the time featuring two fools and the caption, 'We three, loggerheads be'. The third fool is the person looking at the cartoon. This archaic reference might be better served by setting up a 'See No Evil, Speak No Evil, Hear No Evil' monkey tableau, the keepers obliging the child-like Antonio.

**186–194**  The cries of Madmen 'within' break up the aptitude testing. Since Middleton and Rowley give no details as to where the Madmen speak from it's up to the director and designers to decide whether they were present all along or if they are seen or unseen for these lines. A sense of tension could be maintained throughout the performance if the audience were periodically startled by these outbursts of lunacy, perhaps from out in the house of the theatre itself.

Very few spectators will get the cheese joke about Welshmen notoriously loving 'Parmesan' but luckily the amount of pure crazy talk here dispels any deep alienation for the audience. The reference to 'Bedlam' would have met with knowing approval at the time by a Jacobean London audience that would have been familiar with the place and its practices. Today the name is synonymous with a general chaos. Traditionally the 'fools' were kept separate from the violently mad so a division between voices from opposite sides of the stage would be historically accurate as well as dynamic.

**195–207**  Alibius exits with a reminder for Lollio to keep an eye on Isabella. Lollio gives Antonio a declension lesson on the Latin for 'stupid' and hopes 'to get credit by' him, perhaps meaning that his plan is fully cooked to use Antonio as a tool for sexual blackmail with Isabella.

## Act II

### Act II, scene i

**1–26**  Beatrice and Jasperino enter '*severally*' or from opposite sides of the stage. She has sent for Alsemero's friend to deliver a message to Alsemero but exactly where are they in the castle? This scene might be set in Beatrice's bedroom if her awakening sexuality is to be underlined, but the idea of servants and strangers coming and going there would seem to make that unlikely. If one wants to play up Beatrice's 'innocence' a more neutral location would better serve, one where De Flores could enter without overt erotic suggestion. Spaces could become more and more confined as the story unfolds, from public rooms in the castle to the eventual confinement of Alsemero's closet in Act Five.

Beatrice's soliloquy on the superiority of Alsemero over Alonzo is another chance for the audience to be drawn along into choosing her new lover over her now troublesome fiancé. She stacks the deck against Alonzo and tills the soil for a radical solution in 'Some speedy way' to be rid of him.

**27–51**   As if Beatrice summoned him with her reverie, De Flores enters to subject himself to the sweet torture of her disdain. It's unclear when Beatrice actually notices him so there may be a long period (during his aside) for him to peep at her. She might be in an erotic daydream about Alsemero or a dark sulk about Alonzo and fail to see De Flores because she's preoccupied. Or he could be in some part of the stage that makes him 'invisible' to her but seen to us (like the 'inner above' of Elizabethan stages).

'Some twenty times a day – nay not so little –' is his estimate of the number of brushes with scorn he submits himself to.

What is the root of her aversion? No one else in the play is so put off by De Flores' 'dog face' as she is. He describes himself with 'I must confess my face is bad enough' which either lends credence to the argument that he's ugly or that De Flores has bought into the belief that because he's from a lower class he is automatically unattractive to his betters. Although he describes what other ugly people look like (and yet still find love), he never tells us just what his physical afflic-tion is. Just how ugly *is* De Flores and to go further: what is 'ugliness'? The audience is hearing it from the ugly man himself and he works hard to convince us he's worthy. De Flores argues that another, uglier man can find 'the grace of beauty to his sweet', so why shouldn't he live in hope that Beatrice might turn her 'blessed eye' upon him. That eye may be her affection (making him romantic) or her vagina (making him a rapist) and it's up to the actor and the director to decide what type of stalker De Flores is. This choice dictates whether this is delivered as a self-deprecating stand-up comedy routine or a bitter screed.

The revelation is dropped that he used to be a gentleman but no clue is given as to just why he was 'thrust … out to servitude'. No back-story is supplied as to just what happened to make De Flores fall. Was he a victim or caught red handed doing something shameful?

**52–93**   The first in-depth exchange between Beatrice and De Flores sets up her major problem: 'This ominous, ill-face fellow more disturbs me / Than all my other passions.' Is it possible to hate someone who does not obsess and ultimately excite us? De Flores revels masochisti-cally in the storm of Beatrice's disgust and offers 'true service' (with a sexual entendre) while drawing out his inevitable dismissal. There is a flurry of shared lines here, i.e. short lines that run into one another so that the characters finish each other's thoughts and begin to overlap. This is very close to naturalistic speech and begs for speed and heat of exchange. Beatrice may be physically pushing De Flores out of the room or attempting to leave herself, but in any conflict the actors must be *attempting to get something from their partner*. De Flores clearly wants to prolong his conversation with Beatrice and it's a stronger choice for her if she desires some piece of concrete information from him rather than just wanting him to leave her alone. The stakes are high if, for example, she wants to hear news from him that Alonzo is unable to keep his engagement to her. As well as plotting out a character's motivations, the actor and director often chart what a character *thinks will happen*. By identifying a high stakes hope, a character can be knocked down when reality blindsides their expectations.

When De Flores says he always seems 'To be i'th' way still' he may in fact be too close to Beatrice, smelling her or even closing in for a kiss. If this happens then she breaks the tension by ordering him to leave, which he doesn't do right away. In his aside (Beatrice may be composing herself after her fury), De Flores compares his stubbornness to that of baited bulls that were set upon by dogs as entertainment during this time (here at Paris 'Garden'). Even if a bull survived the assault by killing the dogs, he had to come back again another day for more torture. De Flores takes heart in the fact that other women have worn themselves down 'As children cry themselves asleep' with chiding ugly men before ultimately sleeping with them. He strives to convince us (himself) that he has a chance with a woman who merely protests too much about the thing she actually desires. De Flores is biding his time, waiting for Beatrice to exhaust her control of her own life. He may have seen what's happening with her affair with Alsemero and can predict she's headed for a fall.

As he leaves Beatrice senses the danger De Flores embodies, but is the 'trembling of an hour after' she feels the result of love or hate for this man? Up to now he's seemed like a supreme annoyance to her but here he's identified with 'danger'. De Flores graduates from cloying pest to a dangerous force, like sex and violence. Her erotic signifiers (i.e. gestures, tone of voice) might be working here to show a new kind of relationship forming.

**93–103** Compared to the 'small disturbance' of De Flores, Beatrice rates her antipathy towards her fiancé as 'Affliction's fiercer torrent'.

This is where her contrary nature could signal that she's lying to herself about De Flores, forced to compartmentalize her feelings and attack a problem she can actually do something about by having the valet sacked.

With his brother Tomazo along for the ride, Alonzo is warmly greeted by Vermandero. Alonzo says he prefers Beatrice's father's favour over a 'treasury of honour'. It's clear he's courting the father and not the daughter (who he doesn't even bother to address here unless it's with a non-verbal signal). Vermandero warns his daughter that her wedding day is swiftly coming (along with her resultant loss of virginity) and underlining that it's his prize to bestow upon Alonzo. She is allowed no voice to publicly express her cold feet for Alonzo and warm heart for Alsemero. She's forced to be an actor with Alonzo (here in pantomime) and whether she's warm or plastically artificial towards him is an important choice. How Alonzo receives her (charming or awkward?) dictates whose side the audience might reasonably take.

Beatrice pulls her father aside and silently entreats him to buy her more time before the wedding. Their brief 'dumb-show' during the de Piraquo brother's argument might be either subtle and reveal nothing or it could be a manic pantomime of Beatrice's feigned terror of her approaching wedding night. The latter would set Alonzo up as booby ripe for duplicity as he stands there chiding his concerned brother for being a poor scholar of love.

It doesn't take Beatrice long to convince her father but does she have a plan yet? Are thoughts of murder percolating by this point? The choices made in playing the role of Alonzo create a strong foil for the audience's perception of Beatrice. If he's a sap or a spoiled prick then we can't help but rally behind Beatrice's motive to marry for love, however spur-of-the-moment. If Alonzo is a well-mannered, good-looking chap it's harder to sympathize with Beatrice. Alonzo has very few lines and almost no action besides proving himself the unwitting gull by ignoring his shrewd brother's entreaties to beware his fiancée. A strong choice made in this small but pivotal role affects the whole plot with his upcoming murder. Alonzo is basically a 'glass half-full' optimist and says and does nothing overtly stupid. A sympathetic take on him may be a more literal reading of the text but with it comes a hardening of Beatrice's persona.

**104–122**   The beginnings of a heart-to-heart conversation between the de Piracquo brothers illustrates the kind of unheeded counsel we know well from the plays of Shakespeare (e.g. Friar Lawrence's in *Romeo and Juliet*). The reasonable (cynical?) brother, Tomazo, warns the upbeat Alonzo about Beatrice's 'small welcome', a clue to how Beatrice should greet her fiancé. The groom sees nothing sinister in her wish to earn a 'reprieve' for her 'maidenhead' and he goes along with her request. This is a rare slowing of haste in a play of ill-considered, passionate decisions.

**122–155**   Beatrice and Vermandero exit, allowing Tomazo to entreat his brother to speedily dump his fiancée, divining that she loves another man. His speech describes Beatrice's heart as a changeling, something that can be swapped for a false affection, just as a fairy child can be exchanged for a human one, wreaking havoc on the family that is duped by it. Tomazo's 'And how dangerous' is a short line that suggests a pregnant pause for effect. It echoes the tingling of danger Beatrice feels for De Flores but Tomazo fails to convince his brother, a victim of 'love's tame madness'. All of the lovers in this play practise their own kinds of denial to proceed blindly toward their intended targets.

### Act II, scene ii

**1–40**   Time passes but this scene might easily be set in the same place with the sense that it's almost continuous. With the flurry of events it's vital to drive the story forward here so the audience has no time to catch its breath. This scene could be played in a secret part of the castle since Alsemero should not be seen consorting with Beatrice. Foreshadowing her desire for Alsemero, Diaphanta admits Beatrice's preferred suitor. She evokes 'danger' again, a word now used by all of the characters who will soon perish from it. Her flirtation ('Complete gentleman!') may position her as a rival for Alsemero's affections. Beatrice's 'I have within mine eye all my desires' and her employment of holy symbolism bring the lovers back to the blissful state we first met them in back in Act I. It's only a glint of sunshine, however, as reality brings back the clouds. The 'poison' of her 'enemy' Alonzo (compare to her earlier take on De Flores) and the hateful 'command of parents' threaten to ruin their coming together for ever. This is a beat where the actor playing Beatrice might perform her as a spoiled little princess, stamping her feet in frustration. Her wishful thinking is passive and seems to demand that Alsemero make everything better for her. Conversely, a womanly frustration is also possible, one where Beatrice is enraged by the lack of agency she has in choosing her own destiny. That may be a revisionist take on seventeenth century womanhood but a more familiar story for a modern audience than a world where a woman's virginity was bought and sold like a commodity. Either way, Beatrice's motivation here is to get Alsemero on her side against Alonzo but when he offers to challenge her fiancé to a dual she changes her mind. She doesn't like the risk; she'd rather send another on a suicide mission since 'Blood-guiltiness becomes a fouler visage'.

**41–56** In a major revelation Beatrice is kicking herself for almost throwing away the opportunity to use De Flores as a murderer. She makes a big rationalization, comparing her manipulation of him to a doctor's use of poison to fight another poison. She's so consumed with the new scheme that she can't hear Alsemero's attempts to snap her out of her reverie. Beatrice advises Alsemero to sit tight until the time is right just as she's about to launch headlong into a hasty decision that will change everything. There may be a kiss as he leaves or she may have moved on already to thoughts of De Flores. An aborted kiss here might be the first signal of Beatrice's declining interest in Alsemero.

**57–69** In another indelible duet Beatrice overcomes her aversion to De Flores in order to make a pact with him to kill the unwanted Alonzo. If this is played as a love–hate relationship then she must push through the danger of love for him as much as sublimating her hate. The trail of breadcrumbs she follows is a series of discoveries that prove De Flores worthy of her trust. A more straightforward reading is that she truly despises the servant and is purely using him to get her desire. This may well have been what the authors intended but since actors and directors are interpreters of malleable material, they must look for clues in the text and make the strongest decisions possible in order to serve the play.

Because De Flores has witnessed this rendezvous (and we might assume all Beatrice's others) with Alsemero he has no misconceptions about her lack of faithfulness; in fact he is content to be one of her many lovers since 'She spreads and mounts then like arithmetic'. His desire for her is not dampened despite seeing her as a 'sutler to an army royal' or camp prostitute. Is this cynicism or blind love?

Beatrice makes a pre-Freudian slip when she decides she can 'serve my turn upon him', meaning use him as a pawn as well as sexually. Now that her true nature is revealed to us we see her to be the greater cynic. Misdirected to believe she's a romantic just looking to be with the boy she loves, the seeming truth that she's a ruthless user hits all the harder.

There has been much debate on just how much Beatrice is actually attracted to De Flores and, if so, when exactly she becomes aware of this root of their tension. The play is filled with reassessments by the unlikely pair that bring them closer together. This scene crackles with sexual tension if Beatrice is wrestling not only with her desire to get De Flores to agree to murder Alonzo, but also beginning to discover her own dangerous attraction to a desperate man.

**70–97**   For the first time during the play (and, we might assume, ever) Beatrice uses De Flores' name to address him. The effect is ecstatic for him and he's 'up to the chin in heaven'. There is real potential to humanize De Flores here in his playing of these earnest asides. Rather than a rapacious rapist, he can appear positively head over heels in love. When Beatrice praises his 'pruned' face she may just be pretending that she finds him suddenly sexy, but what if she's actually having a revelation and seeing him for the first time? This would substantiate De Flores' earlier claim, one Beatrice repeats, that many women rail against 'a hard face' until 'It mends still in opinion'. She tells him 'you were not wont to look so amorously', a double meaning if she hasn't noticed how he's been leering lustily at her but also stronger for Beatrice if she's being honest and he does look a little better to her. This exchange could be played as series of discoveries where she loses sight of her desire for Alsemero as she truly sees De Flores for the first time. She blames his former ugliness on 'the heat of liver' but this was also believed to be the physical home of one's desires so it's another subconscious slip. Every word she says sexually excites and flatters De Flores and he swoons to report, ''Tis half an act of pleasure / To hear her talk thus to me.' The scene is more vital if Beatrice is experiencing actual epiphanies here rather than purely manipulating him. Earnestness of intention allows the audience to be won over to the side of a character that, no matter how duplicitous or unforgivable their actions seem, strikes us as a breathing, fallible human being in search of their own truth. Think of the serial killer whose family leavens or completely forgives them their trespasses due to the fact that they know and love them. An audience that believes in the reality and passion of Beatrice and De Flores here is likely to invest in their journey to the play's end.

There is a physical game being played here and the staging can go as far with the players drawing dangerously close only to part, relieving the tension for a moment before building it up again. The weakest positioning on stage is the 'safe' or everyday distance between two players. Maximum tension is earned from extreme distance or proximity. Touching releases much of this tension since it banishes the *potential* for contact with its actuality. Beatrice only touches De Flores for a moment ('She smells all amber!') and their ensuing distance ('I'll make a water') allows the charge to rebuild in intensity.

Beatrice segues from the 'hardness' of De Flores' face to that of his 'service, resolution, manhood'. All of her words are thinly veiled references to sex and its attendant body parts. She builds him up with flattery and excites him erotically in order to soften him up for the favour she's seeking; but how much is she speaking from a place of awakening to her desires in response to his charms? De Flores continues her double meaning with his 'the honour of a service' meaning both his will to serve her as servant and as lover. His 'So happy as that mounts to' and her 'We shall try you' take the entendres as far as they can stretch. There's really little left to do but fall into each other's arms here as part of her ruse if she did not change tactics.

**98–113**   Now that she's heated him (and herself?) up, Beatrice uses a sighing gambit, switching up her acting ability in order to make him ask her what's wrong. It's a classic passive–aggressive move that still works for most couples today. The inclusion of this moment in their 'conflict' actually makes the two appear like an old married couple more than antagonists. Inherent in Beatrice's argument is her very real desire to have the 'soul of freedom' that came with being a man at this time (contrasted with her virtual imprisonment in her father's castle). Another indicator that he's not your garden variety rapist is De Flores' very real concern for what's afflicting Beatrice's heart here. There's a great bit of frustrated expectations humour to be mined from his delivery of 'Nay, that's not it' when she wishes she were born a man. Leavening the intensity of these dramatic scenes with humour is a great way to purge them of the melodrama that, when overwrought and pushed, can cause them to devolve into soap opera.

**114–132**    De Flores demands that Beatrice 'claim so much man in me' and so we see what were often a woman's only two choices in this period: follow a man's orders or manipulate them as pawns to get what one wants. Beatrice is a master of the latter (having practised on her father?) but little does she know she's playing this game with a sociopath with nothing to lose. Or does she subconsciously know what she's getting into? It can be argued that Jacobean writing was 'pre-psychological' but the works of writers like Shakespeare and Donne show a knowledge of human nature and behaviour that goes deeper than the morality plays of the medieval period.

'There's horror in my service, blood and danger,' Beatrice warns De Flores, but is she so naive as to fail to see this as a call to sex as well as murder (even tender Juliet knew what was waiting for her once Romeo climbed her balcony)? De Flores takes everything she says sexually and she might mistake his erotic greed for an avarice for gold, thinking his 'need is strong upon him' (which it is, but not for money). He begs on his knees to 'serve' her and it's a thrilling image if she exploits his position by playing with his face while he's conveniently at crotch level. 'Belike his wants are greedy,' she tells us and this doesn't sound like financial talk. Beatrice might join De Flores on the floor to show how serious she is in the pact. When heard through De Flores' ears every word she speaks is erotic and the (unintended?) offer of her 'precious reward' (virginity) is in the bank. For De Flores 'the thought ravishes' and he imagines he will soon ravish Beatrice. Whether she's truly aware of what's being negotiated here or slowly coming out of a fog, the audience discerns the way things are going. Whether they look forward to the inevitable or dread it is all in the playing.

**133–146**    A swift series of short and shared lines describe Alonzo's death with the passion of fevered intercourse. It's really more of a negotiation in the taking of a girl's virginity, she asking him to 'Be wondrous careful' and he claiming her fears shall 'ne'er rise to hurt you' (ironically, just as he's rising from his knees).

The haste of this exchange is the haste of bad decisions and pacts that confound the characters of this play. De Flores cannily rushes the resolution of what will happen to him after the planned assassination. Beatrice looks forward to being rid of both Alonzo and De Flores but perhaps her 'loathing' for the latter is because of the overwhelming feelings he elicits in her? Would less passion and more time for thought and repercussions have made everything work out?

Here she coins the term 'dog-face' for De Flores, perhaps completely restored to her former, imperious self now that she has resolved her action of securing him as a hit man. Inserting a short pause here before exiting could underline the previous whirlwind of the negotiation and her confusion as to what she's really gotten herself into. If Beatrice has relinquished some of her high status to De Flores she might demand more sympathy and understanding from us.

**147–153**   De Flores either imagines or has just observed the kind of 'wanton' woman whom he is sure he can sexually satisfy once he has earned her reward. To him she is an 'odd feeder' or woman who praises bad food before devouring it. Is this cunning man blind to Beatrice's aversion and just seeing what he wants to see in her? Or have her signals of honest attraction been too obvious for him to miss? If she appeared to falter in uncertainty in their exchange he could pick up on this and make his strong argument that the harder they come, the harder they fall.

**154–165**   The fly, Alonzo, lands squarely in the spider De Flores' web, with a request for a castle tour that will conveniently place the two men alone together in a spot suitable for murder. Rather than beat around the bush with a scene where De Flores must cunningly manoeuvre Alonzo into place, Middleton opts to cut to the chase and the game is on. The writer's constant use of haste traps the characters in their own ill-considered choices, while the audience doesn't have time to dwell on their lack of shrewdness either. The shared lines here shows how matter-of-fact and blithe De Flores is in setting up the murder. Every line seems to include parenthetically 'No problem!' and it misdirects the audience as well for an act of bloody viciousness.

De Flores' parting line ('He's safely thrust upon me beyond hopes') is to us and cries out for a 'Look how easy *that* was!' glance to the audience.

By this point in the play if the audience isn't hoping for De Flores to get the girl then something is lost. While the piece can be played as a cautionary tale about avoiding partnering with sociopaths, a deeper read involves the impossibility of resisting animal attraction. If De Flores lacks that attraction and is purely a source of vitriolic disgust on Beatrice's part there's nothing motivating us to hope they get together, for better or worse. We may be praying they get together so they can go 'straight' and run away from the oppressive castle together. Or we might wish for a Bonnie and Clyde shootout and grisly end to two outlaws. Either way we hope fervently something happens for them as a couple because as free agents they hold no magnetic force. It's only as a duo that they hold a charge.

# Act III

## Act III, scene i

**1–24**   The stage direction at the end of Act II, '*In the act-time* De Flores *hides a naked rapier*', may come directly from the original prompt book since it seems tailor-made to cue a specific actor at the time of the original production. In private theatres during Jacobean times there were act breaks filled with music. This strange stage direction may have been an indication of a seen action during the interlude or a note that the actor should hide his sword in the 'inner above' for the pending Act III murder scene.

Because the break between Acts II and III feels like such a 'jump cut' in a film, it's often where directors choose to insert bits of the madhouse scenes, which can seem overlong when intact. A sense of tension can be built from stalling the death of Alonzo a little longer. De Flores appears nervous or feigns incompetence with his keys (great stage business built in here) as Alonzo praises the 'most spacious and impregnable fort', echoing not only Vermandero's control of his daughter but Alonzo's own inability to take the virginity of his unwilling fiancée. This is all small talk anyway since all we're thinking about is that this character is a sitting duck about to get killed.

This action was most likely originally staged with the actors going from the 'inner below' up to the 'inner above' via an offstage staircase (or vice versa since Alonzo's murder happens in a 'vault' which may imply an underground space). A modern production could easily use an onstage staircase but creating the sense of claustrophobia inside the narrow walls is a challenge. Transparent walls and reverberant microphones would be a technical solution or perhaps the narrow walls are only the offstage ones. Assuming there are no madhouse scenes inserted here, a pregnant pause (line 11) with no one onstage could turn the screw of tension before the men re-emerge from another door.

De Flores divests Alonzo of his sword claiming the passages are too narrow again mirroring the unmanning of Alonzo, who will never enter Beatrice's passage.

While De Flores hints that Alonzo will soon see a place he never imagined (i.e. death), the latter reveals that he has told everyone he's taking a gondola ride. A convenient alibi for the killer: this is too easy! The way the actor playing De Flores conveys how he's feeling is vital here. He might be enjoying the thrill of the kill or be a dead-souled sociopath just getting the grim job done. The former calls for more audience engagement to 'bring them along' for the fun. This also brings up the idea of black humour in Jacobean revenge tragedy. How much the audience should be encouraged to giggle at this macabre set up to homicide is a choice that must be made. Sympathy for Alonzo, an unfleshed-out character we've barely met, decreases empathy for De Flores, our hero or anti-hero. If Alonzo is someone we can enjoy, on some dark level, seeing cut down then black comedy wins the day. The inverse can slide into two-dimensional melodrama where the too-good innocent is cruelly slain by the too-bad villain. Much of the leavening 'grace notes' of the Jacobean tragedies are moments like these where we find fun in gruesome catharsis. All work and no playfulness make these dramas overwrought and hard to suffer through.

While reviewing the battle station or casement in the wall (these may be 'implied' by the actors looking out into the audience) Alonzo is repeatedly treated to veiled references (though obvious to us) to his impending death by De Flores as in his foreboding comparison of the sound of this castle's 'ordnance' (cannon) to the 'bells of great men's funerals'. How thick is he laying it on here? Is Alonzo perhaps starting to get nervous that something's not quite right or is he mowed down while blissfully unaware of any foul play?

**25–30** Stage combat ensues in which De Flores repeatedly stabs Alonzo. Is there grappling and spraying blood or does the victim go down without fanfare? The director and fight choreographer decide on the level of gore here. The stabbed Alonzo is baffled and finds no explanation from De Flores for his motives in this 'work of secrecy'. Unlike some stage deaths by stabbing where the victim goes on to deliver a long speech while he bleeds out, Alonzo expires quickly. Chances are that his wounds were to vital areas like the neck and heart. As far as storytelling is concerned, Alonzo may just be the first push that upsets the whole house of cards. This is a convention used in many plays of the period (e.g. *Women Beware Women*, *'Tis Pity She's a Whore*) and rather than pausing to eulogize the first victim, the murderer usually sprints on to the next act of violence.

**30–36** Alonzo's diamond ring catches the crow-like attention of the murderer's eye and harkens back to Beatrice's image of a diamond shining in the darkness. One of the most famous set pieces in the play is the removal (and later presentation) of this finger unwilling to 'part in death' with its jewel. There's a cynicism here worthy of a play with two sociopaths for the heroes. That a bloody diamond ring is more important than a man's life is a clear comment on the kind of society the Jacobean's were critiquing with this dark material.

There is no stage direction describing the onstage removal of the finger but that doesn't stop many directors from depicting a gruesome amputation with appropriate sound and visual flare (perhaps even with De Flores' teeth) for the audience's enjoyment. Rather than dwell on the horror of his act, De Flores' 'speedy course' is to cover his tracks so he won't get caught. His dry, business-like approach to cleaning up after a murder could be played as ghoulish fun or as distasteful reflection on the mind of a serial killer.

### Act III, scene ii

**1–11** Back in the asylum Isabella is kept caged by her older husband's cunning servant. Entendres abound as Isabella's need for some meaningful activity ('doing') is interpreted as a desire for sexual high jinks by the lascivious Lollio. Here to 'pipe' means both singing and fellatio and brings the play firmly into locker room bawdiness. 'Pinfold' is both a prison for livestock and a place for a penis. The chauvinism is extreme here, a more grotesque version of exactly what is happening to Beatrice in the 'castle' plot: a woman bought and sold as a commodity by callous keepers. Isabella wishes to 'be doing something' just as Beatrice has taken matters into her own hands. The asylum is the 'funhouse mirror' version of the castle but it can let us draw deep conclusions about the opposing choices the parallel characters make.

The question again is just how far the performer must go to make the more archaic bawdy humour land. Just how much touching and gesticulating is required to make a word like 'pinfold' have meaning to a modern spectator?

Isabella may be pacing restlessly and her motivation might be to get Lollio to set her free, even if only temporarily. Lollio may be engaged in a madhouse related task (e.g. repairing restraints, washing blood off the walls) or he may be petulantly sitting back with his legs up, watching his charge like a hawk. The latter sort of choice makes his character more predatory and ill-chosen for the job of protecting Isabella's chastity.

**11–19**  Another round of 'madmen' vs. 'fools'. The subject as to whether one can tell one from the other comes up again and again. The ultimate theme seems to be that we are all mad and foolish when driven by lust, a state Lollio would surely like to see Isabella succumb to so he could blackmail her. He entreats her to 'be half foolish too' since she's already half mad by sleeping with her husband. His motivation is surely to lure her into sleeping with him. Lollio might just be in search of the money he'll gain as her pimp but it lowers his stakes if there are no emotions, even purely lustful ones, on the line here.

**20–35**  'The pleasure of your bedlam' has a fun double meaning as Isabella may be flirting with Lollio, requesting both his gossip about the 'last come lunatic' and the implied thrill of 'bed-lam'-ing the warden. Isabella is clearly going stir crazy and is intrigued by the idea of a sexy young lunatic. This scene mirrors the one at the end of Act Two where Beatrice flirts with De Flores in order to get closer to Alsemero. How much is Isabella just looking as an outlet for curiosity and how much is she on the hunt for a virile new suitor? By misdirecting the audience here it could be made to look like Isabella is not ruling out Lollio as a suitor too.

Does one play Isabella as an innocent to contrast with Beatrice's sensual cunning or is the mirror of the subplot more fully realized with a similarly conniving Isabella? Either way, she longs for more knowledge of a 'proper body ... without brains to guide it' unlike her elderly husband, all brains and (we may assume) no sex appeal. Lollio plays the pimp and hints that this 'understanding madman' is just play-acting his way into her vicinity. Does he misinterpret her flirting as interest in him?

**s.d.** There's an awkward little pause here where Lollio goes off stage to the get the madman Franciscus. If this is a true moment of silence, how does Isabella spend it? She might be primping to look good, rolling her eyes in despair, or giving the audience a mischievous smile to let us know she's ready to match wits with her keeper. It's up to the director whether to exploit this pause (an editor states Lollio '*enters presently*') and use it as a short snapshot to develop Isabella's intentions.

**36–59** As Franciscus is drawn on by Lollio from the 'mad ward' side of the stage we don't know that he's a 'counterfeit' madman. The actor playing him might set up the scam right away in his 'How sweetly she looks!' as a lucid aside to the audience, dropping his cuckoo character for a second and letting us know he's just acting. He then unleashes a slew of pithy, archaic references that, while probably not gleaned by a modern audience, at least play as loopy doggerel. Or it might be stronger to reveal his sanity later and set him up here as a true madman thereby casting doubt over *every* character's mental health. Are the madmen sane and the presumably sane, like Beatrice and Alsemero, truly mad?

Fransicus may be dressed as a clownish version of a scholar or as a dissolute poet since his discourse is so erudite. Isabella pities this 'proper gentleman' rather than laughing at him, perhaps suggesting how one might play the 'counterfeit madman', e.g. as a tragic, lost soul rather than a ranting maniac. It's apt that Franciscus was supposedly driven mad by love since it is certainly the cautionary tale of the main plot of this play. Here the clowns of the asylum satirize the very real dilemmas of the castle-dwelling aristocrats. Also alluded to is the most classic 'passion breeds madness' play, Shakespeare's *A Midsummer Night's Dream*. It's no coincidence that Titania and Oberon, made famous by Shakespeare as faithless lovers, are summoned here by the would-be cuckold-maker, Franciscus. The 'madman' calls Lollio Diomed, a character in Shakespeare's *Troilus and Cressida* who woos and wins the 'faithless' Cressida.

Isabella naively rationalizes Franciscus' madness by diagnosing that 'his conscience is unquiet'. Perhaps she refers to her own lack of freedom and romance and is tempted by the newcomer? Is there a friction between them that warrants more attention than she'd normally give a real madman? Or is she just playing games to kill time in a joyless prison where nothing ever happen?

Another choice to be made is just how much Franciscus is signalling his sanity to Isabella while laying the madman routine on thick for Lollio. The warden seems to believe that this madman is dangerous since he threatens him with his whip. Or is he just playing his part in the charade? The actors should be clear on their intentions so that the audience is given the clearest sense of the 'rules' of this antic game.

**60–76** A series of very short lines (though not begging for pauses as in blank verse) create a 'Who's On First?' vaudeville effect here. Again the references are classically archaic: unless the audience knows the details of the Tiresias myth they may be in the dark here. The upshot is that Franciscus is 'blind' with love for Isabella. Leave it to Lollio to find a vaginal reference ('eye more than a man') in the discourse.

**77–93** Franciscus slips into blank verse here in a veiled message to Lollio that the two might both enjoy Isabella sexually. For a modern audience this may need to be explicitly acted out to be made clear. Lollio clearly dislikes the idea and drives him away with his 'poison' (whip). From Isabella's description we can infer that Franciscus has grown violent in his speech, perhaps becoming over-zealous in his enacting of tearing 'their wolvish skins' (scratching Lollio?) and saving 'the sheep' (humping Isabella's leg?).

Franciscus continues the Titania imagery with a paraphrase of the Faerie's lines upon putting the Queen to bed in *A Midsummer Night's Dream* (thereby setting her up for a wild fling with the ass-headed

Bottom). This would have been a fresh reference for a Jacobean audience but some 'fairy' acting (a high voice or flitting about?) might refresh the memories of a modern audience of where the quotation originates. The beat ends in a tacit agreement between the men to assist Franciscus into his 'mouse-hole', with obvious double meaning. How much of this does Isabella catch?

**94–106** While frustrated with the forwardness of Franciscus, Lollio still sees fit to invite the 'changeling' Antonio in for more quick banter (most likely from the opposite direction of Franciscus' exit due to the separation of Fools and Madmen wards). Lollio's 'you may play with him, as safely with him as with his bauble' is yet another archaic reference that might require a gesture or prop to clarify the entendre ('bauble' being a euphemism for penis as well as a fool's wand).

Here Antonio acts as a classic fool by telling the complete truth but in such as way as to baffle his interrogator, e.g. when asked by Lollio how long he's been a fool Antonio tells no lie with his 'Ever since I came hither'. A vaudevillian call and response delivery may work again here, this time with Isabella as the 'straight man'. Since there are many opportunities for this device the brevity of this exchange could already be part of an established patter.

**107–111** Interrupted by offstage madmen (perhaps firing make-believe guns; 'bounce' being an archaic reference to gunfire) Lollio is called off to settle them. Was the disturbance instigated by Franciscus, since he just exited and surely wants to draw Lollio away from his charge? Franciscus could either be in collusion or working counter to Antonio in attempting to bed Isabella. Lollio's being called away on business actually sets him up as the cuckold in another layer of the 'Farmer's Daughter' story, a plot switchback set up strongly if we thought Lollio was the young lover we should be worried about.

A modern production could make the madmen visible here and Isabella's allusion to the disturbance coming from 'the upper room' may be a sly reference to the theatre boxes and could allow for the madmen antics to be staged out in the house.

**112–128** Blank verse replaces prose (with a pregnant pauses in Isabella's 'Well, sir' and 'Ha!' short lines) as Antonio reveals he is a 'changeling' or imposter. All of Isabella's lines are brief here, indicating amazement and perhaps an itch to learn more. She certainly never calls for Lollio's protection. With poetic acumen Antonio suggests that all paths lead to an affair with Isabella, sanctioned by Love (Cupid) himself.

**129–143**   The kiss here could be sweet and innocent or grabbing and lustful. Isabella has a strong reaction but it's certainly not an attempt to escape or call for help. Antonio's entreaty that she might forget his 'outward follies' and see 'within / A gentleman that loves you' might be a line delivered by De Flores to Beatrice if he had Antonio's boldness. The concept of beauty lodged within an unsavoury frame is established in both plots. Antonio might be on his knees here in an echo of De Flores during the murder scheme. Both men are willing to go to any lengths to please their objects of desire. While Isabella denies Antonio further discourse she does not reveal him as an imposter. Just what is her motive for letting him stay on at the asylum if not to see more of him in the future? She's clearly not entirely innocent but how tempted is she?

**144–150**   Antonio perhaps references the mad Ophelia in *Hamlet* upon switching back to his disguise as Lollio enters. He might also enact some Ophelia-esque business by passing out 'flowers' to his audience, Isabella, Lollio, and even the real audience.

Has the warden watched their secret exchange like the observant De Flores? He seems to test her affection for Antonio like a conscientious pimp. The verse reverts to prose with a sense of low bawdiness restored. With her 'Passing well' Isabella shows that she's interested in Antonio and that he may 'come to something' if he plays his cards right (perhaps with an encouraging look to the faux fool there). This might also be a warning to him that he's playing with fire and bound for the gallows if he tries anything with her.

**151–162**   A maths lesson is interrupted by an offstage madman's cry, 'Catch the last couple in hell', which comes from the game of 'barley-brake' in which hand-holding couples were placed in 'hell' and chased other couples to replace them there. It's an apt image for the lovers in this play and a strong stage picture that would be well mined by a director here or elsewhere. There could be an area of the stage that represents Hell that is alternately populated by Alsemero/

Beatrice, Jasperino/Diaphanta, Isabella/Antonio, Iabella/Franciscus, Diaphanta/Alsemero, and Beatrice/De Flores (De Flores will bring the reference back in V.ii). Franciscus may have started this game to help his buddy Antonio return another pass at Isabella.

**163–183** Alone together again, Antonio and Isabella shift back to more romantic verse and, despite sharp words of admonishment from Isabella, Antonio snatches a (seemingly uncontested) kiss. Antonio compares the kiss to that of Hercules' labour of snatching golden apples from the dragon-guarded orchard of the Hesperides. Lollio definitely catches them in the act here but remains outside their action, allowing the lovers to continue in verse while he (Lollio) bandies prose asides. Isabella is more concerned about getting caught by Lollio than of breaking her marriage vows. She has seen the 'giant' observing their tryst but how much she fears him versus believing she can control him is unknown. Antonio speaks in synchronicity with De Flores with his 'in your eyes / I shall behold mine own deformity / And dress my self up fairer'. Again, the attraction to ugliness and danger that Beatrice is struggling with in the main plot is replayed here in a comedic way. But does that lower the stakes in any way? If Alibius would kill Isabella for cheating are the stakes any lower than Beatrice's entangling herself in a murder plot over forbidden love?

**183–191** Lollio fittingly cries 'Cuckoo, cuckoo' both for the cuckolding couple and the madmen as they enter '*above, some as birds, others as beasts, [uttering fearful cries]*'. This was originally from the 'inner above' of the Jacobean stage and the image is a strong representation of the fevered passions of the onstage act of adultery. It is also our first view of the lunatics as performers (again, changelings) who 'act their fantasies in any shapes/Suiting their present thoughts'. How are they any different from the shape-shifting Antonio and Franciscus or the false-appearing Beatrice Johanna and De Flores? They might even appear more and more throughout the rest of the play as the sexual high jinks heat up. Representing the Furies of Greek myth, the Insane could be employed to ratchet up the unnerving, out of control nature of lust's triumph over reason. Or this display of the bedlamites might even evolve into something lovely and pure rather than a fearful dance of death. Isabella might even be moved (she clearly doesn't fear them) and taught by the honest 'schools of lunatics' to rethink her dalliance with her handsome intruder. Whether this is a morality play or a prurient portrait of a world without boundaries is up to the artists to interpret.

**192–209**   Lollio removes Antonio with a prophesy to Isabella that the fool will 'put you down one of these days', surely looking forward to his pimp's cut of the action. Isabella, mirroring Beatrice, realizes that despite her incarceration in her asylum (castle), much erotic mischief can be enjoyed by a beauty that attracts suitors through the very walls of her prison. This doesn't seal the deal as to how to play Isabella but it does show that she's no innocent as to how the world works.

**210–228**   Lollio tries to rape Isabella, using the blackmail of her overheard conversations with Antonio. Quoting his 'deformity speech' verbatim it gives a sense of how to stage Lollio's previous exits; he needs to be close enough to hear their words and perhaps has never really left the stage. He may even attempt the same suave moves Antonio employed to steal his kisses from Isabella, only to have her put up a fight. To contrast the romantic nature of Antonio's wooing, Lollio's should be obscene and clumsy. When he talks of 'deformity' there's the sense that he possesses the real kind of ugliness, one that a simple change of costume won't wash away.

**229–237**   Isabella gets on her high horse and switches to verse with a sanguine counter-threat. This is no naive waif and her resolve mirrors that of the street-fighting tactics of Beatrice. Isabella is willing to sleep with Antonio in order to put him in her debt and kill Lollio. While not a direct juxtaposition to the castle plot it's clear that the blackmail scheme is very similar to Beatrice's willingness to pay/sleep with De Flores in exchange for vanquishing Alonzo. Lollio makes it clear that he wants a share of the action in exchange for keeping his mouth shut.

**238–269**   Isabella's luckless husband, Alibius, enters and doesn't take the hint when she entreats him to lock her up for safekeeping (from her own desires and those of others). Instead the doctor eagerly describes the gig for which his fellow clueless father/husband Vermandero has hired the bedlamites. They'll be the entertainment for his daughter's upcoming wedding, thus introducing the first crossover of the two plots. These stories have so far been playing out in 'separate rooms'. The idea is that the lunatics will appear on the third night of celebrations in 'an unexpected passage-over', a drive-by freak show to thrill the wedding guests. Alibius has higher plans of an ambitious dance piece that, if not perfectly in synch, will at least delight the spectators with its bold reach. Lollio is optimistic as he has many fine dancers among those in his care who have danced their brains down into their feet. He and Alibius may be enacting a dance here as they scheme up the choreography that will bring a pretty penny their way at the expense of the dignity of their 'commodity' (patients). One wonders how Isabella perceives this new event and how it will affect her disguised suitors. Is she pleased that the inter-lopers will soon be disgraced or can she be looking forward to his test of their romantic mettle, i.e. if can they remain in character despite this indignity? How does she really feel about her husband's profession? Is this fun for her or is his 'fine trade' a disgusting reminder of just how low she's fallen by marrying an exploitative quack?

The two-dimensional schism in playing Isabella is clear: she can be a saint if played without a sex drive or a whore if she entertains the notion of cuckolding her elderly husband. But what if she's warring with both options? While it would be easy to make Rowley's subplot a frivolous cartoon and part of the reason it's so often cut down or excised entirely, a deep reading of Isabella's motivations could make her story as engaging and upsetting as her fellow 'prisoner', Beatrice. The lack of Middleton's cosmic poetry makes the lunatic plot a more difficult sell in terms of presenting three-dimensional, breathing characters we can root for but Rowley's dirty jokes and coltish sensu-ality are the hooks which sugar-coat the pill and keep us engaged. This plot is often played as occurring in a brutish nightmare world where men dominate an oppressed woman. What if it were treated instead as a sparkling comedy where the sharp heroine undermines the males' efforts by using her mind as well as her sexuality? If she started to lose her well-defended heart in the process to one of the suitors the tone would come closer to a Jane Austen novel than the morality play Hell it most often resembles. While the latter is a gritty, thrilling option, our connection to our heroine Isabella is dimin-ished in that she becomes purely a victim rather than an active agent manipulating a cracked system. This also points to how Beatrice should be played and asks how akin the two protagonists should be.

As they mirror images or opposites? Do we learn more from two contradictory facets of 'women in prison' or by placing them side by side, despite the broad class gap between them, and seeing their similarities under erotic pressure?

## Act III, scene iii

**1–24** Vermandero has been charmed by Alsemero: clearly the latter's tactic to hang around the castle has worked. There might be a secret signalling between the would-be lovers here. Echoing the previous scene, Beatrice is content that her lover has infiltrated the house, here disguised not as a madman but as an unassuming soldier-sailor with an interest in castle architecture. She 'by degrees works out her freedom' since she feels she can't be honest in her true feelings about Alsemero vs. Alonzo. There needs to be a repressive force at work here to strengthen her argument for conspiracy. Without a sense that Beatrice is as much a caged bird as Isabella she merely becomes a 'bad woman' and much of her dramatic power is diminished. If Vermandero is clearly uninterested in what she thinks or feels then our sympathy is on her side. Contrasting the darkness of what she hopes is her suitor Alonzo's 'eclipse', she attributes light imagery both to Vermandero's 'liking' and her own love. This latter illumination is movable like a spotlight rather than a steady beacon, as proven by her lack of remorse over the deed – contrast this with Lady Macbeth's madness-induced guilt over her part in her homicides.

Speaking of *Macbeth*, De Flores enters with 'My thoughts are at a banquet for the deed', a reference to the bloody post-banquet homicide rendered by the Thane for his ambitious wife. These lines, while not indicated as an aside, can be delivered directly to the audience. If he gives them to Beatrice then a choice has to be made as to whether she understands his meaning or misses the drift of his scheme. Beatrice's 'Is it done, then?' and De Flores' 'Piracquo is no more' are more sharp *Macbeth* (II, ii) references that point to a growing intimacy between the conspirators. The fevered shared lines and long pause after line 24 also echo Shakespeare's tragedy. That Middleton chooses a seasoned, married couple as a template and not a mismatched pair of rivals like Isabella and Angelo in *Measure for Measure* (a play Middleton may have had a hand in writing) indicates the level of comfort that may have insinuated itself into this relationship.

Again, where does this take place in the castle? The following conversation is so shadowy and secret that it might be in a private space where no one can overhear the conspirators. Yet it must begin in a public space since Alsemero and Jasperino are getting a castle tour, so this dangerous negotiation may in fact be taking place in a space where anyone could overhear them and ruin everything. Their ability to whisper depends on the size of the stage (or use of microphones) but the sense that they could be discovered at any moment ups the stakes enormously.

**25–38**    Beatrice is thrilled to tears and shows no remorse at the fate of her former suitor, a man who has never, as far as we know, said an unkind word to her. This might be where the tide turns against Beatrice and her darkness overwhelms any sympathetic qualities. Does she have no conscience or is she able to compartmentalize her emotions to the point where her excitement for being united with her true lover overwhelms her immediate understanding of what's really happening? Another pregnant pause follows after her short line 'For me?' as she waits for De Flores' love 'token': Alonzo's severed finger replete with diamond ring. The wait here is built into Middleton's 'verse blueprints' with Beatrice's short line and begs for a very slow reveal of the finger. After the blistering speed on the terse lines above this pause builds a delicious tension that is as seductive as it is disgusting. One of the kinkiest moments in any play, the exchange predicts the Grand Guignol craze in early-twentieth-century France and the modern horror film. Shakespeare's *Titus Andronicus* and Ford's *'Tis Pity She's a Whore* prepare one for this erotic exchange of body parts where a primal gift of flesh represents the actual sex act. By what degree is Beatrice horrified, fascinated and even turned on by De Flores' love token? Perhaps a series of reactions is the best possible choice. We only know for sure that she doesn't run shrieking from the room as we might expect a young, sheltered girl to do. De Flores is macabre and cavalier in his bestowing, as if the amputation were a tender afterthought like plucking a daisy, a mere trifle proving his esteem. He also resembles a cat that brings a dead animal into the house as an offering to his mistress. De Flore's movement here could suggest the feline, enticing Beatrice towards his desired end.

**39–56**    Getting down to business, Beatrice raises the issue that 'the keeper has his fees'. Do we hear the unwitting reference to the other keeper, Lollio? She offers the ring (again, like Isabella's protected 'ring') as partial payment but how much does she realize that the 'soon applied' fee will be her virginity? Surely she is aware that this man lusts after her and has no scruples about taking whatever he desires, regardless of the consequences. Yet if she believes they have an agreement and that her status over him controls her father's servant, Beatrice has nothing to worry about. If she thinks he's just after the money then she can continue her denial regarding her mounting obsession with despising/loving him. A major choice needs to be made as to whether subtext will be played here (i.e. she knows he wants sex but can't let him see that) or if she means what she says (i.e. she truly has no idea what's coming next). Both choices have inherent high stakes and electric tension but they suggest radically different ideas about Beatrice's character and motivations.

De Flores pushes the issue, insinuating sex with his double entendres 'capcase', 'worm', 'performance', 'warm', and 'service'. The actor playing Beatrice chooses here how much she attempts to repel De Flores (as Isabella does Lollio) or signal her tacit consent. She may just be testing his intentions and forcing him to show his hand since he's never overtly stated his intentions to sleep with her. Or she may be playing it cool because she fully expects the financial bargaining to end in mutual satisfaction.

**57–80**   The pause after De Flores' short line (57) signals a breakdown in negotiations. In an attempt to pay him off, Beatrice incites De Flores' rage. If he really heats up here ('Now you move me!') she might become more cold to counter his intensity, witnessed in her short, confused lines. He cites putting his own conscience on the line by murdering Alonzo himself, something he claims he would never have done for gold. That he ever had any conscience is debatable but his emotional blackmail puts Beatrice in 'a labyrinth' where she doubts for the first time the prudence of her part in the homicide. She claims in an aside 'I know not what will please him' and because they are her private thoughts perhaps we should believe the power of her denial. Whatever her budding desires, she did not expect this kind of reaction from De Flores.

**81–87**   When she tells him he must name his price and leave for ever he counters with the fact that she will have to flee too. A very long pause might come after her simple, 'I?' or it could be done as a swift eleventh syllable to the line (81). This is an enormous event and a game changer. Whatever Beatrice's plan must have been it surely didn't include de facto banishment from her comfortable lifestyle. The writing is on the wall as De Flores explains that his absence would incriminate her immediately. She's trapped. How much is she scheming for an exit strategy or allowing herself to give in to his proposition that they 'stick together'? The phrase itself is a jarringly modern-sounding one that also summons the sex act. His 'engaged so jointly' also suggests that they are married by the deed while feeling quite naughty.

**88–100**   De Flores goes in for a kiss. Is it aggressive or like a tender lover? Beatrice's 'This shows not well' seems to indicate that she's not appalled yet and so he's not thrusting himself on her without chivalry. When he tries again, however, she tells us 'I doubt him!' where 'doubt' is akin to 'dread' but with much milder connotations. In a pitiful attempt to repel his advances Beatrice warns De Flores to 'take heed ... of forgetfulness', easily countered with his reminder of her own spotty memory of their sanguine deal. Much of this exchange is in the form of shared lines that call for immediate cue pick-ups and a racing pace. His 'I'm in pain / And must be eased by you; 'tis a charity' doesn't conjure the image of a rapist so much as an unrequited lover begging for solace. He may be trying to control his temper in order to convince her he's a gentleman and worthy of her love. De Flores invokes 'Justice' and his use of 'blood' is at least a triple entendre meaning her high birth, bloodthirstiness and the impending stain of her lost virginity. Yet if he were truly in it only to steal Beatrice's virginity and be done with her would he take so many pains to explain his motivations here? It's clear that he loves her and respects her enough not to drag her off for instant gratification.

**101–119**   Her 'I dare not' precedes her 'I never shall' and might signal that she's tempted but her virginity (required for her wedding night) and other dangers (e.g. discovery by her father and Alsemero) prohibit her from acting on her desires. She wishes she that she could reverse 'What has been spoken' so that temptation might be erased. Rather than obliging her, De Flores launches into a lustful screed describing his adamant need for his 'pleasure', only after which will he be willing to reckon financially. His sexual obsession for her is poetically, graphically rendered here. Is he vulnerable or terrifying in his confession? While the former may actually evoke sympathy from the audience, the latter may raise the terror stakes for her. Somehow De Flores has been assured of her virginity and that is what he prizes foremost, like a vampire feeding on purity. Why is her virginity so important to him? There's a connection to 'ownership' here that mirrors that of Vermandero and Alibius. The men in this play are obsessed with possessing something untouched by others. They are so worthless inside that they regard what they own as the measure of the man. Conversely, if De Flores is the play's hero it may just be that he needs to be the most special person in Beatrice's life. If she had already given herself to another he'd be willing to go home with his ill-gotten money. Evidently it's only a physical purity that De Flores values. By this point Beatrice has surely proven herself to be as ruthless and 'wicked' as he.

**120–131**  Ascending her high horse again, Beatrice claims she cannot imagine how he might 'make his (Alonzo's) death the murderer' of her honour. Citing the difference in their classes and her (laughable) modesty, Beatrice is surely grasping at straws. Her argument ('twixt thy blood and mine') becomes repetitive with that of her earlier protestations so a director may choose some form of a chase here where De Flores makes his move toward finally possessing her. Again the question of location is crucial: do they have to keep their voices low or can the actors explode freely? Does Beatrice try to signal for help? Is there a couch or bed where De Flores might take her right there and then?

**132–140**  In the most apt expression of these erstwhile lovers' condition De Flores states that Beatrice is his 'equal' in conscience (or lack thereof). They really are two halves of the same ruthless, passionate being. Does this make them ideal partners or magnets of the same charge, destined to repel one another? He identifies Beatrice as 'the deed's creature', a woman who has traded any birthright or father for the agent of her desire, De Flores. She has been banished from 'peace and innocency' and made one with a 'foul villain' by becoming a 'fair murd'ress'.

**141–160**  De Flores repeatedly calls Beatrice a 'whore'. Does he believe this or is it sour grapes for the fight she's putting up? Either way he demolishes her 'modesty' defence by proving her changeable in her affections. Again, he can be vulnerable and close to tears here or savagely on the offensive, battering her defences with heartless words. Another changeling besides Beatrice appears in De Flores' image of Alonzo being 'changed now' in death. Comparing himself to darkness itself in his plans to taste her sweetness, De Flores threatens to sabotage her possibilities of marrying Alsemero if she does not consent to his wishes. He is suicidal, raving, admitting that his life is hell without his object of desire. When she finally begs him (on her knees, mirroring his kneeling earlier) to take all her wealth in exchange for letting her keep her virginity intact, De Flores delivers an ultimatum that nothing will buy it from him. He has taken over the role of owner of her body.

**160–170**    Line 160 is a short one and suggests a pause as Beatrice bursts into tears. She cites a biblical curse, harkening back to the first scene of the play, contrasting a pre-Fall Eden with the loss of innocence in the introduction of the viper (also a phallic image of impending intercourse with the snake De Flores). He assures Beatrice that she arranges her own 'peace' with 'this yielding'. His 'how the turtle pants' is a tacit stage direction regarding how closely he holds her, but whether this panting is from terror or excitement (or both?) is open to interpretation. Perhaps Beatrice Johanna fully faints here, either from an emotional breakdown or to absolve herself from her desires. She may struggle violently with him if this is interpreted as a rape but her silence may signal a complicity that screaming for help would surely absolve. In Jacobean times the depiction of the sex act would take place offstage but in a modern production the bed might be there for all to see the night of joy or terror the two lovers share.

# Act IV

## Act IV, scene i

**s.d.**    A dumb-show, common to the fourth acts of many Elizabethan and Jacobean plays, truncates time so the discovery of Alonzo's vanishing and Alsemero's marriage to Beatrice are shown with no need for verbal explanation. There is a lot of room to play directorially with a dumb-show and it can range from a swift thumbnail sketch that advances the action to a chance for a grand pageant full of detail and choreography. It's a good place to check in with the characters and see what they're feeling through observing their faces and body language rather than their words. Is Beatrice degraded or satisfied? Does Alsemero suspect that things have moved too fast for foul play *not* to be involved? Is Vermandero truly pleased with second best (Alsemero) for his daughter and (more importantly) his fortunes? What about Jasperino (jealous?) and Diaphanta (lustful?)? We are told that a trailing De Flores is pleased with having de-virginized the bride. He doesn't get to enjoy it long before he is menaced by the ghost of Alonzo. How is the ghost staged and represented? Does he keep popping up at inopportune times throughout the rest of the play, beyond where he is mentioned in the dialogue? Alonzo is given short shrift as far as haunting time in the text but a director may decide to employ him more as the screw turns and the characters sink deeper into their self-made quicksand.

**1–16**  Beatrice, just outside of Alsemero's closet' or study, delivers the longest soliloquy of the play and follows the classic structure of solving a problem aloud: introduction of a difficulty, wrestling with it, and its resolution (or lack thereof). She reveals how she has been 'undone ... endlessly', using the term 'fellow' for her lover De Flores, a word also meaning 'accomplice'. Her undoing is sometimes interpreted in performance as sexual exhaustion (and can even be played for comic effect) or that she has been multiply raped (for tragic significance). Her language is not as despairing as the latter would warrant, however (a pause before 'undone' would no doubt get a laugh) and her fear is more of getting caught by her new husband than for the peril of her body and soul. She has clearly lost any romantic disposition for her approaching wedding night and scrambles to find a way out of it. Her husband has become her adversary ('He cannot but in justice strangle me') as her nemesis becomes her ally. She compares her gambit with Alonzo's death and her virginity to a game wherein Alsemero is a 'cunning gamester' and she's playing with a 'false die' (with a triple entendre on dice, death and orgasm).

**17–52**  Wrestling with the problem in Alsemero's study, Beatrice falls into a wildly Jacobean plot device. Alsemero's amateur chemistry set of sorts represents the period's craze for alchemy and similar mumbo jumbo. This makes for a delicious bit of sleuthing on Beatrice's part as she stumbles on a home pregnancy kit and, worse yet, a virginity test. This 'physician's closet' could be a fun design challenge, mystical and arcane with the possibility of hidden panels and cubby holes. This is such a preposterous plot twist that it could either be played for 'camp' factor or exactly the opposite, deadly serious. There is an advantage to playing it for laughs in that it misdirects the audience away from her role as a murderer and dwells instead on her need to cover her tracks as an unwilling (?) adulteress.

**53–99**  When her maid, Diaphanta, opportunely interrupts, the soliloquy's resolution comes into focus. When characters arrive at just the right time it's often a device for something terrible to befall them, as with Alonzo previously.

Beatrice proves herself a cunning actress by convincing her maid (and especially her 'nice piece') to stand in for her on her wedding night. The mistress uses her outward fear of exposure as motivation for her feigned terror at the thought of her approaching coupling with Alsemero. Diaphanta, for all her coquettishness and entendre-slinging, is avowedly a virgin and can't believe her good fortune. In her private asides she reveals how hungry she is for the new master of the house. Her 'Would I has such a cause / To look him too' might even be said directly to Beatrice, thereby allowing the mistress to pick up on her maid's covetous disposition right away.

Many shared lines here are a cue to drive this exchange quickly, even overlapping them when possible. The fourth act of any five-act play is an ideal time to put the pedal down and begin racing towards the conclusion.

Just as Beatrice has employed De Flores to kill for her she hires Diaphanta to 'lie' in her stead, both verbally and sexually. The cautionary tale is clear: even passive aggressive murderers/adulterers are guilty. Beatrice's overriding motivation (what Stanislavsky termed the 'super-objective') is to get what she wants without getting her hands dirty. Diaphanta is justified to wonder 'how the world goes broad / For faith or honesty' when she's presented with the 'have her cake and eat it too' hypocrisy of her mistress. How naive versus street-smart should Diaphanta be played? Both are strong character choices but the former makes her fate more sympathetic than the latter. Also, a Diaphanta who is just pretending to be innocent is not a bold contrast to Beatrice's play-acting. The comedy is more acute if the maid's 'Your honorable self is not a truer' comes from a genuine gullibility and we laugh because we know better. Beatrice has a moment of premonition about Diaphanta's 'quick' disposition in her 'Bad enough, then'.

**100–127**   During this vetting process Diaphanta may be unsuspecting in drinking from 'Glass M' or, if she's played as a tough cookie, she may slam the 'shot' like a veteran drinker, thinking it's alcohol to brace her before she's searched by the 'forewoman of a female jury'. Here is some rare slapstick humour in the tragic main plot replete with Diaphanta's sneezing, hysterical laughter and, finally, deep gloom. In a quip on singing/copulating Diaphanta accepts her wedding night stand-in assignment with 'I shall carry't well, / Because I love the burden'. The entendre may not translate here but could be shored up if Diaphanta sang those lines. She looks forward not only to the fun in bed with her 'trick', Alsemero, but the thousand ducat fee she'll be able to use to pad her dowry portfolio.

## Act IV, scene ii

**1–16**   This entire scene, most likely in a public space in the castle, blasts along at a breathless pace as the threat of detection of Alonzo's murderers comes home to roost.

We learn that the madhouse changelings, Antonio and Franciscus, are in fact gentlemen in Vermandero's court. Their absence throws suspicion on Vermandero and his 'honour' is much more on his mind than his feeling any great loss for his would-be son-in-law. His motivation is to clear his name by laying hands on the fugitives. The threads between the two plots start to draw together as Rowley, it's posited, handles the first 16 lines before handing the play back to Middleton for the rest of the scene.

**17–34**   The 'too hot' Tomazo, Alonzo's avenging brother, accuses Vermandero of brokering a 'hasty tie' which points to Alonzo's 'most certain ruin'. Vermandero artfully deflects the blame back on Alonzo who he condemns as faithless, having fled from his duty to wed his daughter. This tells us that no body has been found yet. Vermandero proves as hasty as his daughter in making rash decisions before considering the consequences. He assumes Alonzo took 'his flight so unexpectedly', never considering that some grave fate may have befallen him. Truth versus falsehood is set up as the major antithesis here and continues through the next beat.

**35–58**   Vermandero is replaced in the same breath by De Flores who only heats the dialogue further, witnessed by the even shorter shared lines. De Flores is reminded of Alonzo's murder by his proximity to his brother. His motivation is to get away ('off') from Tomazo while appearing completely innocent of any wrongdoing. His acting prowess is strong and Tomazo naively trusts in him despite De Flores' veiled warning, 'I think none worse than myself'. The classic trickster always signals his bold intention and the dupe never picks up on the true message, as with De Flores' seemingly jocular description of Beatrice as a slut (like 'most ladies'). Tomazo may be deceived by the harmlessness of De Flores but he's right about his 'wondrous honest heart' in that he has told no lies. His motto might be 'I think none / Worse than myself'.

**59–77**   A third rival enters, Alsemero, and further fans Tomazo's motivation to discover the murderer of his brother. The initial use of monosyllables between Tomazo and his brother's rival Alsemero indicates emphatic chilliness here. It may be a cue to slow things down to underline the danger. Tomazo's reference to swilling wine may be a clue to play Alsemero as drunk here. There are more hot-headed shared lines as Tomazo makes threat of a duel, but it won't be on this 'solemn' wedding day.

**78–106**   Blind to the reality of his role in this mess, Alsemero states, 'My innocence relieves me'. He may not know what's about to hit him or, like his bride and father-in-law, he's well-matched in denial and solipsism. He similarly urges haste in Jasperino and ignores his friend's entreaty to keep a cool head about the news that he's over-heard Beatrice and De Flores in intimate conversation. The image of owning a woman through control of her virginity is continued in Jasperino's revelation that the trysting couple's words were 'Like those that challenge interest in a woman', meaning De Flores has been speaking like he 'owns' Beatrice. Shaken in his belief that it's him alone who controls his new wife, it's now Alsemero's turn to demand that Jasperino drop this hot topic, feeling acutely that 'truth is full of peril'. He is immediately willing to doubt his beloved's fidelity, revealing the shallow depth of his infatuation with this woman he barely knows. This is a big emotional shift for him, from completely convinced that any hanky-panky with 'poison to her' De Flores is out of the question to damning her to exile. The switching point is in the revelation that Diaphanta has heard the two lovers when they thought no one could hear them. It's a difficult transition but one that might well be set up in earlier scenes. Anywhere in the first three acts where Alsemero might be portrayed as charming but capricious, a creature of changeable fidelities (like Beatrice and Vermandero), would set him up for this hot-headed transformation.

**107–121** In a rare moment of restraint in this play of passionate motivations, Alsemero decides to use his virgin detection kit to test Beatrice's faithfulness. He does not wish his best friend to judge him by his 'passions' so he tries to put the breaks on his rage. Ironically he still proceeds like a rash fool rather than stooping to actually communicating with his wife. He does have cause to be confused and wary, however, as he reveals Beatrice, through her agent Diaphanta, has entreated him to come in total darkness ('obscurity') for the newlyweds' 'sweet voyage' together. This is not the behaviour of his forthright, flirtatious love interest in the first half of the play. We know by this point that she is far from the 'timorous virgin' she's pretending to be and Alsemero could use this gross discrepancy to fuel his jealousy.

**122–129** Upon seeing his bride, Alsemero dismisses of any further belief in her guilt. She appears so chaste and guileless that he flip-flops once again. Is Beatrice a great actor or is Alsemero truly blinded by her obvious wiles? A combination of the two is possible, too, as in *Othello* where Othello is blind *and* Iago is an accomplished actor. The balance will affect how tragic or comic their exchange plays.

**130–150** In one of the most rapid-fire series of shared lines in the play, Alsemero administers the virginity test and Beatrice 'hand-somely' feigns the effects as she witnessed them in Diaphanta. Is her acting here believable or a laughable (to us) re-enactment of the real effects as exhibited by her maid? Again, this is about giving in to camp versus 'selling' a ridiculous plot twist with a poker face. The stakes are life-or-death for Beatrice and the true interest for her character is how successful her playing is rather than how realistic. She triumphs in that Alsemero is now totally convinced of her innocence. What does Jasperino, having overheard the lovers' conversation with De Flores, think? The scene's final image might be Alsemero and Beatrice in an embrace with Jasperino shaking his head dubiously. If Beatrice caught sight of him it would create a tension that she had still more observers of her handiwork to get rid of.

## Act IV, scene iii

**1–27** In the madhouse Isabella, apropos of the previous tableau asks, 'Does love turn fool, run mad, and all at once?' The dovetailing of the two scenes here may almost indicate that the newlyweds' example spurs her desperate query. While they occur in separate locations a director might stage the scenes to overlap here, sharing the space for a moment to underline the parallel struggles.

A letter from Isabella's would-be lover, Franciscus, mirrors his own feigned state: passionately mad on the outside (envelope) and madly passionate on the inside (text). For this particular madman sex with Isabella is his only 'cure', though it appears that he is not alone in this desire. Compare this to his fellow changeling De Flores' cure for ugliness and disdain that he seeks in carnal embrace with Beatrice.

**28–47** Isabella and Lollio agree that if she consents to becoming a healer of fools and madmen that he will get a share of her trade, payable in sex, of course. This is a direct replay of the murder scheme between Beatrice and De Flores, and a physical mirroring in this more sexually explicit 'practice' might be desirable. Isabella remains opaque as to her intentions here, scheming only to 'use' her suitors in the 'fair' sense. Lollio naturally assumes this means she'll 'abuse' them by having sex with them and demands to be first in line to 'fall' on her. The two become conspirators against her husband and exchange 'counsel', an intimate act that gets Lollio revved up sexually. He's chomping at the bit to get his one-woman whorehouse open as he relinquishes his key to his wardrobe (perhaps originally the same area of the stage utilized for Alsemero's alchemical closet).

**48–63** Alibius interrupts Lollio, who may be vividly fantasizing a seduction of Isabella, to check on the status of the asylum inmates' wedding dance. It seems rehearsals have been going well and they are nearly ready to perform. Alibius might resemble another over-earnest amateur director, Peter Quince from *A Midsummer Night's Dream*, wildly nervous and full of trepidation. His fear that the madmen might 'Affright the ladies' also recalls Snug's 'Method' acting as Lion. Lollio, more like Bottom, attempts to calm his boss with his ever-phallic assurance that their 'commanding pizzles' (whips/penises) will tame both the inmates and the ladies. There are one or two that make him 'mistrust their fooling', pointing to his feeling nervous about his first two 'johns', Antonio and Franciscus. Lollio plans to 'instruct them' which most likely includes a threat that they dare not breath a word of their proposed infidelity to the boss. Here rehearsal for the dance is just a smoke screen for the sexual negotiations that have higher stakes.

**64–74** Alibius checks in on his young wife's mood within her 'restraint' (with a slip on the restraints used to tie down his patients). Lollio slyly alludes to the fact that Isabella is finding 'pleasure in the house' and alludes to her needing to trade up to man of greater phallic girth (Lollio) than Alibius. Of course, Alibius detects none of Lollio's irony, mirroring fellow-cuckold Alsemero's gullibility in the previous scene. He is so clueless that Lollio can brazenly mock him as lead by the nose ('like the trunk of a young elephant) and the doctor takes it as pure silliness. Lollio is actually working in Isabella's favour here since her motivation is for greater freedom. Lollio's 'a little more length', however, is surely not a measure of his altruism.

**75–93** Lollio teaches Antonio his choreography while exchanging archaic entendres about dance/intercourse. Antonio is playing with Lollio here just as the latter toyed with old Alibius moments before. This major digression so late in the play might stem from William Rowley perhaps writing either of these roles to act himself. This loopy dance lesson serves little purpose besides providing a broad comic bit to highlight the wily 'Tony'. We don't know if Rowley was a strong dancer but he did specialize in fat clown roles so it could have been a chance for his Lollio to showcase some physical comedy.

**94–114**  More acting ability is shown in Isabella's donning of a madwoman persona to give Antonio some of his own medicine. She compares him to the would-be-bird Icarus, apt since he's about to experience a fall greater than a mere stumble during dancing. Now is her chance to be lewdly suggestive, entreating him to 'tread the lower labyrinth' and offering to 'suck out those billows in thy belly' (i.e. while on her knees, suggesting fellatio). She employs Franciscus' erudite phrasing here, cross-pollinating a fool with a madman. Stage action added by the editor is explicitly called for in Isabella's lines, which demand a physical manhandling of the resistant 'changeling' Antonio. These are hardly the actions of a naive waif, as Isabella seems to have been up until this point. 'He's down, he's down!' tell us Antonio falls and 'thou mount so high' signals that he's risen again. Her motivation is most likely to disgrace Antonio here as she's hoping to either make him cry or throw off his disguise and reveal himself in frustration. The result might be that Isabella can see how Antonio acts toward a woman he's *not* infatuated with. Is he the type of tomcat to take a stranger up on this kind of lewd offer? Rather than purely rubbing his face in the dirt she may in fact be vetting him as a suitor, whether he's compassionate toward the mad, exhibits patience when tested, and can resist carnal temptation. This would be a motivation based on *love* rather than one merely seeking to chase her would-be lover away for ever. Or Isabella may in fact be the one person in *The Changeling* who sees what we see and plays along with her suitors' ruses so she can catch them out in a theatrical way. While the stakes are lower than in the castle plot they are both hurling towards a showdown where justice is tested.

**115–129**  Isabella's test quickly reveals Antonio's true colours. He threatens to kick the demented 'madwoman' in a moment of hair-trigger judgment reminiscent of the 'watchful jealousy' of Alsemero. Yet again the nature of who is a true fool arises as Antonio shows his hand as an imposter in the madhouse. Now that she has ascertained that Antonio's desire is truly skin-deep, Isabella reveals her disguise and flatly shuns his advances. Would she have given in into his desires if he had treated her madwoman persona with respect? If she had begun to feel real emotions for Antonio it would create higher stakes for her character. Or this could be her way of maintaining a higher status over the predatory fools and madmen, Lollio included.

Either way she needs to stay one step ahead of those who would simply use her and move on.

The eye of the beholder is evoked again in her analysis that she has no real beauty for this 'quick-sighted lover' beyond what's in her external appearance. 'I came a feigner to return stark mad' is a wonderful tag line for the play itself: all of the story's changelings reap their final reward in exposure and infamy. Antonio threatens to go truly mad if Isabella leaves him. It appears he's used that ruse once too often. As with Beatrice, he 'cries wolf' and is denied, although he seeks communion rather than escape.

**130–148**   Antonio reveals his disguise to Lollio who claims to have seen through it from the start. As in the 'castle' plot, Lollio (De Flores) offers to abet Antonio (Alsemero) against Franciscus (Alonzo) for Isabella's (Beatrice) affections. There's the insinuation that murder could even be involved, a game changer for this thus far innocuous comic version of the main stories. The plots are now so closely tied that the question becomes how to keep this late scene from being merely a redundant replay of events in Act II. It may be a matter of seeing the story the first time as a tragedy and the second as a farce. This two-sided approach allows a *Rashomon* effect where the audience sees dual points of view, comic and tragic. Or a director might prefer to make this turn in the madhouse story so grotesque that it batters the audience's senses. The repercussion could be that the comedic plot gets scarier than the tragic one. If we relive the same story with demented clowns in a phantasmagorical madhouse it could make the infidelity and murder plot of the beautiful aristocrats in the main plot the more palatable of the two.

**149–191**   Lollio reveals that he knows that Franciscus is also a changeling by reading his secret letter to Isabella aloud when the second feigned fool enters. Franciscus drops his ruse right away and there should be a sharp distinction vocally and physically between the feigned madman and his 'sane' persona, as with Antonio. Lollio sets up a duel between these rival lover-fools. The style is pure Groucho Marx/Bugs Bunny and the two noblemen swallow it hook, line and sinker. Lollio resembles Puck in the mad forest brawl scenes from *A Midsummer Night's Dream* but unlike in that comedy the showdown never happens in this play. It does build an expectation of approaching violence ('he's dead already') and drives the action forward into Act V.

**192–202**   Lollio sets up the financial downfall of one of these feigned fools by agreeing to offer up his fortune to one of Alibius' friends (who could petition to become a guardian of an 'incurable' inmate and help themselves to his revenue). This is one of the most obscure references in the play and there's little chance that any audience member would follow the logic here but it's mercifully just a passing remark to get Lollio offstage.

The act ends with a dress rehearsal of the 'madmen's morris' that never has a chance to grace the wedding festivities in the tragic plot. Is it a shambles, terrifying or actually aesthetically pleasing despite itself? So late in the play it may best be used to spike the energy levels and blast us into the final act, but it could also be a final shot of comedy before the rollercoaster comes down the final hill. Alibius deems the dance to be 'perfect' and this could mean that the spectacle is indeed in great shape or it could land as the punchline to a pitiful farce. This is our farewell to the asylum; does it feel like a wrapping up or that there will be more to come?

# Act V

### Act V, scene i

**1–11**   The clock strikes one a.m. in what is most likely a hallway in the castle. Beatrice's paranoia spirals as she waits for Diaphanta to return from her wedding-night stand-in work with Alsemero. The bride suspects her maid's role in initially inciting Alsemero's suspicion of her mistress's virginity and has no compunction about having her killed since she's proven herself unreliable. Her bloodthirstiness is now her cardinal trait and the actor might be destroying something here (e.g. tearing up flowers, her wedding veil, etc.) or pacing like a caged panther. The parallel to Lady Macbeth is inescapable here as the thirst for murder is unquenchable, but does Beatrice's conscience torture her or is she merely a sociopath? This is a surreal ten lines of dialogue as proven by the clock striking two just seconds after it was one. There's room for reality to be played with here and a dream-like atmosphere to be created from this point on. Maybe it began in the 'bad trip' nature of the madhouse dance sequence and blurred over into the castle plot? Through use of music and a heightened style of acting and movement the play could proceed from 'naturalistic' to 'phantasmagorical' in order to raise the thrill factor and drive the ending home by increasing the audience's engagement. A sense of 'What is going on?', if not too alienating, can be the ideal way to draw us in for the final act.

**12–25** What has De Flores been doing? The actor should always know what happened just before their character enters in order to arrive with a sense of energy and expectation. It's clear that De Flores expects Diaphanta to have completed her task by now but he's dead wrong there. He may have been keeping watch over Vermandero's chamber in another part of the castle to make sure he didn't stumble upon the bed trick. Halting rhythms abound in short lines between De Flores and his lover. This may indicate listening for Diaphanta's overdue return or they might be pauses in which the scheming lovers grasp at what course to follow. Again, they sound like an old married couple with her petulant 'I must trust somebody' followed by his brooding silence. He scolds her for employing a lusty maid when he could have hired a more reliable agent like an apothecary's daughter. There's comic relief in this random line of reasoning that could be mined here to break and then re-establish tension. The preposterous device of the bed trick, used in several Elizabethan plays, might best be played with the highest stakes and swiftness possible in order for a modern audience to suspend disbelief that any groom could so mistake his bride's maid for her mistress.

**26–45** Day is breaking, another surreal truncation of time perhaps denoted by a shift in lighting. De Flores damns Beatrice as 'undone', meaning her scheme, her virginity and, perhaps, her nightgown. In some productions Beatrice transforms from a beautiful doll to a hardened slut after she tangles with De Flores and so she might be falling out of her costume here. She's suicidal with despair and seeks counsel from De Flores (ironic since so much advice has been ignored by all thus far). Again, seeking counsel is an intimate act and the lovers' body language could reflect their new relationship. De Flores, after shutting Beatrice down as she panics, comes to her rescue with a quickly hatched plan during fevered short lines of bickering dialogue. His scheme is to light a fire in Diaphanta's chamber but he forebodes disaster in 'I aim / At a most rich success, strikes all dead sure'. Does Beatrice pick up on this with a shiver? The plan accounts for Diaphanta's being in or near Alsemero's chamber and will also drive her back to her own room.

**46–48**  In a particularly archaic image, De Flores describes his idea: after he's lit a fire in Diaphanta's room, he'll be ready with a gun to pretend to fire it to 'cleanse the chimney', supposedly blocked and smoking. In actuality he'll murder Diaphanta when she returns to her room to put out the flames. How a modern audience might understand this in the telling is unclear so perhaps a re-enactment of his plan is appropriate, maybe even with a real rifle (or broomstick?) at hand to make all clear. This element of the murder plot is perhaps the most confusing and in need of strongest clarification. There's room for some comedy here with Beatrice nodding furiously, accepting a scheme that will sound ludicrous to modern ears.

**48–49**  Conversely, with Beatrice's 'I'm forced to love thee now, / 'Cause thou provid'st so carefully for my honour', there is potential for real tenderness and vulnerability. The two villains have come together in a moment of agreement and love. It's only two lines in an otherwise crazed scene, but they speak volumes about Beatrice's psyche at this moment. Is it a newly realized, deeply felt love or just feverish Stockholm Syndrome talking? The key to this complex character's journey may rest in how those two lines are delivered.

**50–58**  De Flores shrugs off the loving moment to race forward with the plan now that the idea of 'fire purifies wit'. As with Beatrice above, his character could appear as either truly heroic or cravenly scrambling to stick his fingers in the leaky dyke of their crumbling scheme. If it's the former, a slower pace and strong connection between the actors could strengthen their lovers' connection. If the latter, he could be racing to explain his tenuous plan while he exits, not returning the blank admiration of his 'hostage' (if she's playing Stockholm Syndrome). A third choice is that *one* of the lovers is struggling to connect (i.e. truly *in love*) while the other is numb to their attention and unable to return their warmth in that moment. Any of these options makes for a strong statement about the nature of love vs. lust but a strong choice made here effects the rest of the play and all that went before it.

**59–67** Alonzo's ghost, symbolic of their guilty consciences, appears to haunt the murderers. What form does he take? This is a spirit that makes relatively low impact, saying nothing (unlike King Hamlet) and evoking less horror than Richard III's guilt-inducing ghouls. De Flores' 'thou that tak'st away the light' suggests a darkening of the stage that modern productions can achieve. For him the ghost of his victim is 'but a mist of conscience' so it's debatable how deeply he's moved during three lines of the apparition's appearance. Beatrice, left alone by De Flores, further unravels in a 'shivering sweat' as her terror is exacerbated, more by the coming of dawn than by the ghost of her ex-fiancé. There may be laugh line with her 'This night hath been so tedious' in that a whole night has passed in a frenzied 65 lines full of schemes and spectral visitations.

**67–73** De Flores has lit the fire and alerted the house, again earning Beatrice's admiration ('who would not love him?'). Could she have changed her tune so quickly without the seed of love for this man in place from the start? Although she stills finds his face loathsome, she compares his 'service' (with a double meaning of 'sexual perform-ance') to the beauty of 'the east' much like Romeo refers to Juliet as the sun.

**74–81** Chaos reigns as servants scramble to find the fire under De Flores' leadership while Beatrice berates Diaphanta for her mishan-dling of her carnal assignment (with a cheeky entendre on her 'trim work'). She dismisses her maid with 'Your reward follows you', tacitly dooming her to the murder awaiting her there.

**81–104** The utterly duped Alsemero unwittingly states that he 'was coming' when Beatrice 'missed' him, a bawdy joke on one level, but in reality calling for some quick thinking on Beatrice's part. She picks up his thought mid-line as if she were actually there in her bed while he was returning to her. He foolishly deems the 'fire is not so dangerous' while she trembles in his arms. Surely her frayed nerves aid in this performance but do we see a feigned interest in him here? Which man does she really love?

If he has fallen for De Flores then ideally we have too. The actress playing Beatrice has entered into a relationship with the audience where we are her confessors and judges. There's little to like about Alsemero by this point. While we may have been misdirected to like him in the first scene of the play and wish him well in his quest for the woman who so blinded him with love that he interrupted his life to stay and win her. Now that he's achieved his goal there has been almost no understanding or love talk between these newlyweds. The true partnership, almost a marriage, has been between Beatrice and De Flores. If we're hoping they solve this Gordian knot together then Beatrice may be looking to us at this moment for acceptance and help.

Vermandero, the ultimate solipsist, enters and exclaims, 'O bless my house and me!' He and Alsemero are two blind men who can't see their castle of sand falling away under their feet. Vermandero commends the 'piece'-toting De Flores for his ingenuity, referring to this 'dog-face' as a performing 'dog at a house fire', like he's an expert firefighter (although to modern ears he might sound more like a mascot Dalmatian, even more condescending). Beatrice aptly calls her capable lover 'a wondrous necessary man' and prepares the ground for the onlookers to swallow that Diaphanta's offstage murder is a tragic accident, the bitter fruit of her own slovenliness in tending indoor fires. The double meaning is not lost for the audience, who knows the maid has been 'negligent and heavy' while playing with fire tonight.

**105–109**   De Flores returns and reports the death of Diaphanta whom he is quick to mention is a virgin lest any of the gullible onlookers put two and two together. The editor's stage direction indicates he has the body of Diaphanta with him (suggested by 'What's that?') but it might be more realistic for him to simply tell the onlookers she's 'burnt'. It's easier to suspend our disbelief that she's been shot and stowed away than that De Flores had time to torch her and carry her, still smoking, into the room. If the visual image is stronger, then to cloak the bullet wound and hide a hasty torch job De Flores may have wrapped the maid in a sheet that no one cares to remove to examine her gruesome remains. Luckily for him none of the assembled choose to comb through the forensic evidence. He and Beatrice pretend to mourn the person they most scorn at the moment. There might be a quick look of relief between the two now that their cover-up of the bed trick is largely complete. A very quick pace here is the key to stifling questions about the feasibility of these events.

**110–113**   Before she has a chance to exhibit any more of her acting ability, Beatrice's crocodile tears are cut off by Alsemero's entreaty not to mourn. She pretends that his words are enough to cease a stream of what must surely be tears of relief. De Flores might be staring meaningfully at his lover while her husband takes her possessively in his arms. She may be echoing the gaze with a tacit commitment to return to her real hero soon. There is no denying that from here on the lovers are deeply connected and together on the fast track to Hell but there is still potential for the audience to think they might just get away with it. They have covered their tracks thus far and could pull it out if we have faith in them, another reason playing 'the villain and the victim' might diminish our breathless rush to a resolution.

**114–128**   More play-acting as Beatrice pretends to have just learned of De Flores' 'double goodness' in fighting the fire – an apt expression since their entire relationship is built on double meanings and duplicity. She offers to reward his bravery, likely with more of herself, while the blind Vermandero and Alsemero second her. De Flores marvels, amazed by her cleverness and carnality which threaten to eclipse his own. So far it's been his lucky day.

### Act V, scene ii

**1–25**   In a scene that could be staged continuously with the previous one, a misanthropic and revenge-thirsty Tomazo 'think(s) all men villains', vowing to kill the next one he sees. If he wants to murder a scoundrel he has his pick of almost anyone in this play but conveniently De Flores *'passes over the stage'*. The actor playing De Flores must motivate just where he is headed, assumedly in great haste, perhaps even disposing of Diaphanta's charred body. Forgetting his previous faith in De Flores' honesty, Tomazo now names him for the 'venomous' snake we know him to be. His vitriol here may give credence to the idea that De Flores is truly hideous in appearance. He attacks him when the servant attempts to cross the stage again.

**26–42**  The basilisk is again invoked when Tomazo upbraids De Flores for breathing upon him. A fight nearly ensues but De Flores is stifled in his reaction by seeing Tomazo's 'brothers wounds / Fresh bleeding in his eye'. More shadows of *Macbeth* as guilt starts to emasculate De Flores but there's also his pragmatic nature at work as he realizes that Tomazo is subconsciously on to him ('instinct is of a subtler strain'). De Flores avoids Tomazo so that he may live to fight another day, showing him to be either a coward or a 'wise lawyer', largely dependent upon how hot or cold the actor plays this beat.

**43–58**  A pause after a short line on De Flores' exit allows Tomazo to ponder his next move. He decides to avoid any kind of discourse with any man since all men are suspects in his murder investigation. With the unexpected entrance of Alibius and Isabella the two plots directly cross over for the first time. It's a very late point for the dual plots to connect so the mirroring of events and themes up to this point should be underlined to keep the audience equally engaged in both. In *The Changeling* the two plots can almost entirely exist in isolation from one another, witnessed by the frequent cutting of part or the entire asylum story. They share none of the same characters until the very end and even then only in the most slapdash overlap. The madmen's morris in the asylum plot could easily be for a different wedding party that we'll never see and the false blame for Alonzo's disappearance could be cast on Jasperino's sailor helpers in the first scene. The point is that an active juxtaposition of the two plots by the director, designers and actors allows the audience to feel the symbiotic relationship between the two stories rather than become alienated by their overt isolation from one another.

**59–86**  Vermandero is willing to sell his men out now that they've been found and made him look bad. Tomazo is instantly relieved of his undirected rancour despite the fact that the two (we know to be innocent) men have received nothing akin to their day in court. More haste rules the day as Tomazo vows 'like subtle lighting to wind about 'em / And melt their marrow in em'.

This is the pyrrhic resolution to the subplot (except for some formal summing up at the play's end) and leaves much unexplained about Isabella's reasoning in exposing her suitors. While it might be assumed that she never slept with either man, her abrupt ending mirrors Beatrice's ability to play the fink in order to save her own skin. If Isabella truly is just 'doing the right thing' by turning them in, she becomes the 'good' wife to Beatrice's 'bad' one and a black and white morality play is accentuated. Yet if she has a black eye or other indicator of abuse we may assume that Lollio in fact exposed the ruse and Isabella's role in it. She may have been dragged to the castle so that Alibius could keep an eye on her. The nature of her temptation and how she resolves it creates the depth in her role and the audience's anticipation as to what her fate will be. It also allows the comic plot to sour once the life-or-death consequences of infidelity come home to roost, in this brutal society.

## Act V, scene iii

**1–13**   In a room attached to his 'closet', Alsemero's suspicion is again excited after having seen Beatrice and De Flores in the garden (with biblical overtones) with his own eyes. Physical appearance is showcased here, Alsemero finding his once-radiant wife 'ugly' just as she once found her lover De Flores repellent. The 'black mask' is the literal one that she wore for her rendezvous as well as the 'original sin' she has inherited from Eve, the root of her inconstant ways. Jasperino urges him to 'search this ulcer soundly' by confronting her with a deep 'probe', using medical terminology for this amateur alchemist. Alsemero, like the fallen Adam before him, finds himself ruing his 'first sight of woman'. He remains ironically unaware that he was the story's original home wrecker.

**14–20**   Beatrice enters, perhaps still with her mask on or carried with her. Sometimes the character, once clad in white, is decked out in a red gown here to symbolize her shift towards the demonic. She might also be costumed in white so that her violent ending 'reads' from the back row. There ensues a very tense exchange in short lines and monosyllables between the newlyweds in which she wants to make him believe she's innocent and he wants to make her confess her guilt. Two motivations of equally high stakes but she bears the burden of having to lie while he must control his dark temper. Long pauses follow many of the lines as Alsemero attempts to draw Beatrice out to a revelation while she tries to ascertain what her new husband really knows about what's going on. A physical activity for her would assist her in appearing nonchalant. She might be adjusting her make-up or getting ready for bed, anything that would avert her eyes from his condemning ones.

**21–35**  Alsemero bluntly comes to the point by asking if Beatrice is 'honest'. She literally laughs it off as being too general a question to answer with a yes or no. She claims she wouldn't resort to crocodile tears to prove her innocence but we've seen that's not true. Her brazenness here suggests she's evolved beyond the fear she was consumed with at start of the act. Despite her blithe protestations Alsemero calls her a whore and she answers immediately in a shared line, suggesting she's poised for such an accusation (contrasted with a short line indicating a pause for her to absorb this effrontery). She claims that being called a whore 'blasts a beauty to deformity' but it gets to the heart of the matter: this beauty has become warped and unrecognizable due to all the lies she lives by. She puts the blame for her infidelity upon her husband rather than De Flores or herself. Was she always a truly ugly person lying in wait beneath a beautiful mask?

**36–53**  Alsemero claims he will 'rifle' through Beatrice's heart to avoid being caught up by the lies of her 'sweet tongue'. He uses the terminology of seizing a castle or other piece of property, threatening to 'demolish' and 'ransack' her body. Her father's fears come home to roost as the truth comes out, namely that Beatrice was always considered a commodity, first by her father, next her demonic lover, and now by her avenging husband. Her 'easy passage' is both the easily access to her castle and her vagina. She might deliver this with a new found 'impudence in triumph' towards him acquired from her relationship with De Flores and possibly latent from much before that. Alsemero reveals that he witnessed her intimacy with her 'lips' saint' De Flores while she wore a visor (mask) and that she merely feigned her loathing of him to disguise her lust for her servant.

**54–78**  In spectacular form, Beatrice spins his revelation to prove her innocence. She cross-examines her husband in an effort to make him show his hand on just how much he knows. She seems poised with a new lie, ready to deny his accusation of adultery until he presents concrete evidence. Once he's made it clear that Diaphanta had sold her out she counters with the fact that the 'witness' is dead and therefore can't testify against her. She reveals the murder of Alonzo and that in her desperate need she 'stroked a serpent' by employing her hated nemesis. Like a true sociopath, she tells the truth in order to justify her crimes. She twists the murder as a distasteful sacrifice she made to allow their marriage to happen and that her deal with the devil was a vile bargain she had to make. Her 'I did it all for you' excuse falls on deaf ears as Alsemero harkens back to their first meeting in 'the temple where blood and beauty first unlawfully / Fired their devotion, and quenched the right one', a satisfying bookending of the play in which the same gestures from his first soliloquy might be repeated to send the audience back on his flashback with him. His passion for her extinguished, Alsemero now clearly sees his new wife as 'all deformed'. The scales have fallen from the blind eye of the beholder and he thinks he sees her as she really is. In fact he's just substituted another two-dimensional figure for the once he vanquished. The 'good woman' has been replaced by the easily vilified 'bad woman' and neither encompasses the depth of this complex character. Because he rashly courted and illegitimately won this stranger as his wife, Alsemero never had a chance to know who he was dealing with. It's little surprise that these two don't know how to communicate but they in fact have the same values, namely getting what they want no matter what stands in their way. He's a hypocrite and she's a ruthless, but now honest, sociopath. Is it any wonder she's more matched to the 'honest' murderer De Flores?

**78–89**  Grasping at straws as her husband despairs over her crossing a 'dangerous bridge of blood', Beatrice has the audacity to claim that she is still 'true unto [his] bed'. This could be a final lie to deflect punishment but since she's come clean about the murder and adultery is seems odd for her to fib again. It may mean that they are both fickle opportunists who deserve one another. In a modern production she might be negotiating for an open relationship so she can still keep seeing De Flores. This would require the ultimate audacity on her part while perhaps bringing back the sparks the couple had in their first love scene. Alsemero might be flustered by his desire for her as he answers her justifications by locking her up in his closet and now literally becoming her 'keeper'. His 'be my prisoner' reflects the madhouse plot where Isabella is both a treasured jewel and a mistrusted inmate. While the dubious stage direction says *Alsemero locks her in the closet*, the quarto text simply has her exiting here. It might be a stronger move if she goes voluntarily, embracing her new candour.

**89–100** As if on cue, in walks De Flores. Playing it casual when Alsemero mentions that Beatrice commended herself to him, De Flores pretends that she still loathes him. His composure unravels as Alsemero notices blood on his 'band' (collar) and he counters with an uncharacteristically lame excuse. The mayhem of the evening must have taxed his powers of subterfuge. Here he is again echoing the role of Lady Macbeth and her 'damned spot' that will never come 'out'.

**101–114** Alsemero goes in for the kill by forcing De Flores to admit his role in the murder of Alonzo. Alsemero's threat of death is deflected by De Flores' claim that his wife is a whore (in a prettily rhymed couplet!). In true police interrogation style, the partners in crime begin to attack the character of the other while the detective lets them tear each other apart. This confession session might even involve Alsemero pushing De Flores into a chair and grilling him like a cop show. Alsemero finally realizes he's a 'blind' man and damns the lovers as 'fair-faced saints', a testament to their cool under pressure.

**115–121** On cue to dispel the myth that these 'saints' are under control, Beatrice breaks down and condemns De Flores (from '*within*') as a liar. De Flores begs to be allowed to 'go to her' and it might appear like he is either going to console or kill her. It's all the same to Alsemero, who acts as 'pander' and locks the lovers together in his closet. Bizarre behaviour, since one would assume he wouldn't want them to be together, but the jealous husband entreats them to 'rehearse again [their] scene of lust' like Paulo and Francesca for ever damned to Hell (where he claims they are headed). Does he intend to watch them from a crack in the door as they reunite? Or is he going to get a weapon before he's interrupted?

**122–139** From here it is believed that Middleton and Rowley worked closely as their separate plots' characters come together for a wildly passionate resolution. A mass of characters from both plots pile into the room at the worst possible moment, prolonging the tension of the final resolution. The group includes the faux inmates, Antonio and Franciscus, who may have been beaten up by Tomazo. Vermandero's attempt to reveal them as Alonzo's murderers is met with Alsemero's conviction that he currently has the 'more close disguised' murderers at bay. Franciscus calls for 'easy truth' while Tomazo demands haste, representing the two sides of the play's battle between reason and passion.

**140–142**  Beatrice screams from Alsemero's closet (most likely the same inner stage space where her fiancé Antonio was murdered). This is sometimes played as if she is having an orgasm offstage ('Oh, oh, oh!') and who knows just what these 'twins of mischief' have been up to since being locked away together over thirty lines ago. Sometimes it is *their* perspective that the audience sees, i.e. Alsemero's closet is on stage and the other side of locked door is off. This allows us to see the lover's final moves as endgame is reached. They may embrace, kiss, make love, struggle, stab each other, or a combination of all of these in plain view of the audience. If they are obscured offstage the audience fills in the gaps in what they can see and might provide more prurient or violent imagery that can be realistically presented on stage.

**143–158**  The most dramatic moment of the play comes with the entrance '*DEFLORES bringing in BEATRICE* '. Again, urgency is demanded, here by De Flores, if anyone present has anything to say to the dying lovers. Another Fall of Man reference is supplied in his comparing Beatrice to 'that broken rib of mankind'. Vermandero once more bemoans his raided 'citadel' – there is no one of importance in his world beyond his castle and himself. It seems Beatrice finally admits that *she* is the poisonous one, warning her father to stand back or be defiled by her, and that she is akin to bad blood let by a surgeon (a commonplace in the period). Blood here also refers to her noble family, one she has as good as disowned by coupling with a servant. She advises to 'Let the common sewer take it from distinction' as her blood literally ebbs away before her stunned audience. She compares De Flores to a 'meteor' (or shooting star) to which her fate was predetermined (as opposed to a fixed celestial body like those with a happier destiny). The warning sign of her 'loathing' for him was 'prophet' that she should have heeded. Her honour (virginity) is irreparably linked to her life, which is over. Has Beatrice woken up from De Flores' spell here or was it always an enforced relationship? Is her last minute recantation believable or a final ploy to come across as a victim of an intrigue she herself instigated? It's a choice to be made and one more mystery to be grappled with in playing this variegated character.

**159–171** Beatrice comes clean to Alsemero about her wedding-night deception and the death of Diaphanta. De Flores compares his fornication with her as 'barley-break', harkening back to the madhouse game in Act III where couples were placed in a symbolic circle of Hell. Vermandero suggests that they all find themselves there now that the truth is out.

De Flores' admits 'I loved this woman in spite of her heart' and expresses a double meaning since Beatrice seemingly hated him and has no faithfulness for anyone at all. He reveals that he was Alonzo's killer and that it was worth it all for the pleasure of being able to take Beatrice's virginity and with it her life. No one else can have what this frustrated servant fought for and got. Whether this is the end-of-the-line bluster of a man who truly loves or the frank cynicism of an unfeeling sociopath is a decision for the actor, who has decided well before now what kind of lover/rapist De Flores is.

**171–179** Vermandero attempts to have De Flores seized but is thwarted by the villain's 'penknife' with which he ends his life (presumably slitting his own throat) with a final decree for Beatrice to 'make haste'. His 'I would not go to leave thee far behind' is as romantic a sentiment as one can imagine and in different circumstances it would evoke many a tear from an audience. In a hurry to the very end, Beatrice follows him in death with an apology to Alsemero, but how heartfelt is debatable. There is potential for real pathos here if played with honesty and vulnerability. Conversely, if this is a straight morality play the effect would likely be, 'Good riddance!'

**180–195** Vermandero bemoans his own lost honour, clearly more concerned with his 'record' than the horrific death of his only daughter. Alsemero sees the glass as half full, however, and claims that Vermandero's innocence is regained in the death of the guilty, that truth and justice have won the day. Along with Tomazo, the three injured parties seem able to shrug off the loss of Beatrice, De Flores and Alonzo with relatively little anguish, proof perhaps that there was actually small room for affection in their hearts in the first place. There's cold comfort for a morality play now that the least interesting characters pass judgement on the sexy, exciting ones.

**196–218**  Alsemero states the play's themes of inner ugliness that hides beneath outer beauty and servitude that masks malice. His analysis, however, is so obviously laid out with no guilt assumed on his own part that one wonders if he was meant to be a reliable narrator. Lest we were left in any doubt, every character in the play could be named a 'changeling'. Beatrice and De Flores were two imposters among many, just as Alsemero was one as he 'changed embraces / With wantoness' with Diaphanta, and Tomazo who exchanged 'an ignorant wrath / To a knowing friendship'. Soliciting other examples, Alsemero and company learn of Antonio ('from a little ass as I was to a great fool as I am'), Franciscus ('from a little wit to be stark mad') and Alibius (from a 'jealous coxcomb' to a 'better husband'). Vermandero has changed a corrupt daughter for Alsemero, who pledges to be a duteous son. This feels sanctimonious and stiff compared to the excitement and danger the dead lovers brought to the play. Perhaps Middleton is setting these final speeches up as a final hypocrisy, making us long for the wild side where the private lines of asides spoke more truth than these public platitudes. If these 'true confessions' were staged as if each character had a gun to his or her head (after all, three murders have occurred in Veramandero's castle), their hollowness would suggest a deeper, more challenging meaning.

**219–226**  An epilogue spoken by Alsemero entreats the audience not to grieve but rather to show their enjoyment of the play with applause, thereby resurrecting the dead, i.e. returning the dead characters to the stage in the form of actors taking their bows – a goodly device for getting the 'dead' Beatrice and De Flores up off of the stage floor and into line for a curtain call with the other lovers, madmen and fools.

# 3   Intellectual and Cultural Context

'May you live in interesting times.' This phrase may be used as a curse or a blessing and since no one knows for sure where the saying originated we have no context for how it should be used. Whether seen as positive or a negative it's an ideal tag line for the Jacobeans.

How did the state of Renaissance entertainment grow so dark and bloody so quickly? How did they evolve from *Romeo and Juliet* and *A Midsummer Night's Dream* to plays like *The Changeling* that feature casually severed fingers, baroque home pregnancy tests and the comedic exploitation of the insane? While there were precursors to Jacobean revenge tragedy in Shakespeare's *Titus Andronicus*, Kyd's *The Spanish Tragedy* and some cynical set pieces in Marlowe (as witnessed by the bitter hot-poker-up-the-bottom ending of *Edward II*), most plays written by Elizabethans didn't feature casts of characters behaving as cruelly and selfishly as most do in the pre-Interregnum works of Middleton, Webster, Ford and their colleagues. What made Jacobean audiences crave the kind of overt sex and violence we associate with today's mass entertainment?

Interesting times they were. Perhaps a reason *The Changeling* and other dark material had to wait to come into vogue again in the 1960s and 1970s was because that period so closely resembled England in the first decades of the seventeenth century. Queen Elizabeth I's death left no clear successor and began a tide of uncertainty that brought England to the tipping point of civil war. The weak, capricious leadership of the Scottish outsider James I laid the groundwork for Cromwell's uprising and Puritan backlash. Despite plague being frequent the population of London quadrupled between 1500 and 1650, exacerbating the kind of urban tension we see in our modern metropolises. While everyone believed in damnation and feared being cast into Hell for breaking rank with Christian ideals, unsanctioned sex and violence of all kinds were being engaged in and clearly audiences wanted to see it on stage as well. Bear baiting and dog fighting were still popular entertainments just as they exist today (bears vs. dogs being replaced by 'ultimate' human fighters in cages; dog and cock fighting arenas moving just below the legal radar).

*The Changeling* was written during a serious economic depression inherited from Elizabeth's reign but exacerbated by James' fiscal negligence. Religious antipathy raged between Protestants and Catholics in a way that made staying in England untenable for many. The colonies in the New World came into being under James as Puritans fled from this political and religious oppression. The Thirty Years' War, spurred in part by Catholic-Protestant hatred, raged in Europe and despite James' refusal to get involved, almost all of England's neighbours were entangled in its bloody mess including Spain, where *The Changeling* is set. The crowning event of homeland instability was the failed terrorist attempt to blow up Parliament and King James himself at Westminster. The Gunpowder Plot of 1605, attempted by English Catholics, may have done more to rattle the Jacobean psyche than any other event of that period. It cast a looming cloud over the safety of the nation akin to the Cold War's nuclear holocaust anxieties and Vietnam post-traumatic stress of the 1960s and 1970s when *The Changeling* returned to London stages.

In the Midland Revolt of 1607 thousands rose up to protest unfair practices by the aristocracy only to be beaten down with hundreds hanged in retribution. A mini-version of this kind of abuse by a weakened regime was seen at the 1970 Kent State massacre in the US where the Ohio National Guard fired on unarmed protesters. Plays in opposition to leaders and reactionary policies like *Hair* and *US* abounded in the 1960s and 1970s just as Jacobean plays like *The Revenger's Tragedy* featured anti-establishment themes so dangerous that Middleton had to remain anonymous as its author. Assassinations of American reformers (Dr. Martin Luther King Jr., the Kennedys, Malcolm X) and the Vietnam War where there was no credible 'bad guy' fomented the kind of political angst with which the Jacobeans also grappled. While the protest play has become a benignly tolerated facet of twenty-first-century culture, intolerant regimes in countries like Myanmar, Iran,

Belarus, China and North Korea still regularly ban the work of their artists often under the threat of imprisonment or worse.

While the fall of the Soviet Union may have allowed for nearly a decade of unwarranted relief from fears that the world would end by our own hands, the terrorist attacks of 9/11 brought the monsters back into our minds. This malaise has reached an international peak in the close of the first decade of the twenty-first century as fears of terrorism are matched only by a lingering global recession. The Jacobeans feel remarkably contemporary to us because their social, political and religious unrest most closely reflect our own. It was a time when royalty was painfully transitioning from a holy, all-powerful entity into a more moderate, cooperative governor. Rulers became more human in their weakness and indecision, opening the door for kings and queens to be seen as purely figureheads while elected officials who could be easily removed would wield the real power. As the twenty-first century unfolds our leaders are more and more often called into question as fallible people just like us. Much has been made of mistakes and crimes of US presidents Nixon, Clinton and G.W. Bush and British prime ministers Thatcher and Blair, mortals who, while not yet fully accountable, are open to censure by the people they govern in a way that the Jacobeans were experiencing for the first time in English history. The power of public opinion in the form of a stronger Parliament and fears of insurgency shaped how leaders made decisions. This was a bold, new concept, one that provoked uncertainty and fears as secular ideas replaced religious givens. Kings weren't able to evolve quickly enough and civil war resulted between pro- and anti-government factions. That newfound worldview has come full circle in our time when political leaders are treated more often as public servants and the split between fundamentalist ideologies threatens a restaging of the Crusades.

This limbo between innocently being cared for and suddenly being on one's own is the kind of existential dilemma that breeds the need for prurient entertainment. It can be seen in the modern world's insatiable craving for sex and violence as entertainment. As a bad behaviour thriller, *The Changeling* gives a jittery, uncertain audience the wild ride it craves.

Middleton surely apprenticed with Shakespeare and may have had much to contribute to his psychological and challenging 'problem' works like *Measure for Measure* and *Timon of Athens*. He seems to have cut his teeth on plays like these where cynicism and misanthropy trump romance and courage. The female characters of Middleton evolve into deeper, more powerful figures than almost any in Shakespeare. Beatrice is an even match for Lady Macbeth in ruthlessness and willing to do more than Juliet for her forbidden love. Alongside themes of political and religious insecurity, the roles of women (although still played by male actors) became more prominent and dangerous. The times called for an exploration of powerful anti-heroines as things were spinning out of control and London was headed towards a civil war where sexual repression won out over tolerance and liberality. The pressure cooker eventually exploded into the ultimate excesses of the Restoration as typified by Lord Rochester and culminating nearly a century later in the Marquis de Sade. After the work of these explosively erotic and perennially banned writers things would retreat again into another period of modesty and repression seen clearly in the nineteenth century when light operettas by Gilbert and Sullivan and drawing-room comedies were all the rage. A glint of Jacobean themes was again seen in the work of Henrik Ibsen but, while often controversial, these plays didn't feature mutilations and implied wild sex in adjoining chambers.

The Women's Rights Movement, begun in the late nineteenth century, kicked into high gear in 1960s and 1970s where the battle for equal treatment, especially in the workplace, brought great gains for women while misogynistic paranoia lashed back as the accepted family order began to disappear. This fear of female agency, sexual or otherwise, is also a major obsession in Jacobean drama and ties the two eras together. A sea-change from patriarchal ideals (strict rules and distinct gender roles) to more matriarchal ones (cooperation and female self-determination) mark both periods and whipped up a similar sense of excitement and anxiety.

In John Webster's *The Duchess of Malfi* the title character wreaks civic havoc by choosing to secretly marry her steward, a man below her in birth and rejected by her brothers. Her attempts to choose how she lives her own life results in a far-reaching bloodbath affecting more than just her immediate family. In Middleton's *Women Beware Women* another noblewoman, Bianca, similarly marries beneath her only to be manipulated into an affair with a powerful Duke that she later quite enjoys (much like *The Changeling*'s Beatrice if one believes she in fact falls for De Flores). Bianca's hapless husband is disposed of with a minimum of remorse while his lover, Livia, a cynical 'fixer' of adulterous and incestuous affairs, orchestrates a bizarre masque that ends in death for most of the participants. In John Ford's *'Tis Pity She's a Whore* a young woman chooses her own brother as her lover rather than the man her father has staked out for her. Her heart is literally ripped out as a result and becomes an indelible prop in the final massacre. Whether this common Jacobean theme is illustrative of the dangers of letting a woman choose her own partner or proof that an independent woman can't catch a break, it echoes the anxiety of a time when gender roles were changing. On the comedy front, Middleton and Dekker's *The Roaring Girl* stars a liberated alpha female, Moll Cutpurse, who cross-dresses and kicks male butt. Middleton's city comedies like *A Chaste Maid in Cheapside* satirize the Machiavellian crush of urban life where sexually aggressive females abound.

The fact that these plays return to vogue in the heyday of the Equal Rights Amendment and the National Organization for Women is not a coincidence. Many of the plots for revenge tragedies were taken from gossiped 'headlines' (newspapers not yet being commonplace) and sated the public's hunger for stories of 'women behaving badly'. In a repressive society the femme fatale is not embraced and explored except as a two-dimensional scarecrow in a cautionary tale. In a society that struggles to understand a new role for women we see dangerous heroines come to the fore. These are not the mothers and faithful wives of Shakespeare, but the imagined nightmare visions that drive Othello and Leontes into madness made reality. While even a villain like Lady Macbeth controls her husband from within the classic husband–wife dynamic, the women in Jacobean plays shatter that paradigm, opting to reinvent their roles as sexual and political beings. The greatest fear they inspire is that they don't actually need men at all, that they can go it alone if need be. It's no wonder that actresses since the 'rebirth' of the Jacobean play consider these roles to be among the choicest in the Western cannon. Why play a victim like Desdemona or Ophelia when one could go down in righteous flames as Beatrice, Livia or the Duchess of Malfi?

Bra burning and organized women's rights protest in the 1960s and 1970s provoked a backlash of misogynist fear that persists to the present day. At the same time popular culture abounded with vivid portrayals of women breaking all the rules. Dangerous female characters star in *Faster Pussycat! Kill! Kill!* (1962), *Bonnie and Clyde*

(1967), *Foxy Brown* (1974) and *Carrie* (1976); women are unapologetically sexual beings in *Lolita* (1962), *Darling* (1965), *The Graduate* (1967), *Barbarella* (1968) and *Last Tango In Paris* (1972); and traditional family life is subverted in *Guess Who's Coming to Dinner* (1967), *Rosemary's Baby* (1968) and *Bob & Carol & Ted & Alice* (1969). 1973's monster hit *The Exorcist* might be better described as a horrific vision of a teenage girl's uncontrolled sexuality than a religious thriller about demonic possession. Just as in Jacobean tragedy, these women burn too hot for the world they live in and often come to bad ends or are at least chastened and set back on the 'right track'. Whether that's a sign of the basically repressive nature of both eras or a deployment of the classic tragic form (i.e. hubris going before a fall) is open to argument.

Meanwhile, Rowley's subplot is as dangerous and bawdy as only short scenes in Shakespeare (*Pericles, Antony and Cleopatra, Troilus and Cressida*) ever dare to be. The audience clearly changed with the times and was willing to accept more overt sex jokes than in the Bard's time. Nearly every line of the asylum subplot is laden with obvious double entendre and one wonders how thickly this was played by Jacobean clowns. How much did the ear catch and how much needed to be supplemented by imagery? The direct descendant of Rowley is British playwright and bad boy Joe Orton. In plays like *What the Butler Saw* (1969), *Loot* (1964) and *Entertaining Mr Sloane* (1963) he brings thinly veiled sexual motives to the fore and blackly comedic high jinks ensue. Orton's style is descended from the Jacobeans and their obsession with aristocrats acting badly. In the US the work of stand-up comedians like Lenny Bruce, Richard Pryor, George Carlin and Redd Foxx were the closest that American comedy came to the unapologetic bawdiness of the frank Jacobeans.

## Sources: Middleton

An innovation of Jacobean writers (some of whom, like Thomas Nashe, wrote pornographic poems to keep the wolf from the door) was to raid the 'police briefs' for inspiration for their onstage works. Rather than poring through Holinshed, Homer and Chaucer for evergreen tales to adapt, they looked to the 'reality TV' of their day for juicy material. Much like today's crime shows and soap operas whose plots are freshly picked from the headlines, the Jacobean used red-hot scandals to build their most popular entertainment.

Middleton's main tragic plot in *The Changeling* finds its inspiration in two sources. Its characters are all adapted from John Reynold's *The Triumph of God's Revenge against the Crying and Execrable Sinne of Wilful and Premeditated Murder*. Fresh off the presses in June of 1621, this 'tragical history' comes from a series of 30 fire and brimstone stories of 'memorable accidents, amorous, moral and divine' written by one of the advisors to the new King James Bible. Presented as a series of morality plays to 'deter us from this bloody sin' of murder, Reynolds wrote a similar series on the undoing of adulterers. Like modern day tabloids or reality TV, these books lure the reader in with the very prurience that they demonize. Similar to both of those current forms of media it's unknown how much of these cautionary tales are actually based on real events. They are presented as reportage but Reynolds' reliability as a narrator is questionable.

His story that informs *The Changeling* focuses on Alsemero, a frustrated warrior in search of a war who gets sidetracked by the radiant, but utterly modest and pious, Beatrice Johanna while in a church service. The dialogue-heavy exchange in Reynolds is nuanced and sexed-up by Middleton, and while Reynolds is clearly repulsed by the courtship of the young lovers, Middleton misdirects the audience into hoping this sexy duo gets together. In Reynolds Beatrice is not even engaged to Alonzo de Piracquo and, while he's a highly prized suitor in her father's estimation, Beatrice finds him loathsome and never desired him in the first place. The Reynolds tale relies entirely on religious fervour and belief in an 'original sin' to motivate its characters. One of many manoeuvres Middleton makes to increase the ambiguity of his dramatised story is to set up obstacles which deepen the original tale's two-dimensional versions of Alsemero, Beatrice and especially De Flores, who in the original is 'gallant' and never referred to as ugly or brutish. While the original features a deeper back-story and the play-by-play courtship of Alsemero and Beatrice, Middleton recasts the dashing, purely opportunistic De Flores of the original into a shadowy vampire who uses dark psychology to win over Beatrice. If there is any doubt that Beatrice subconsciously desires De Flores, one might refer to Reynolds' version where she eventually makes him her lover without a word of doubt or repentance. The question is how far Middleton would take the metamorphosis of De

Flores when so much of the story remains the same? Is he an entirely new character or still, ugliness aside, based solidly in Reynolds? If the answer is the latter then an initial forbidden attraction could well be the source of Beatrice's loathing of her father's valet. In *The Changeling*, once the hurdles of ugliness and class are negotiated, Beatrice behaves towards De Flores much the way she does in Reynolds. In the original she beds him whenever her husband goes out of town, motivated by Alsemero's insane jealousy (he cages her for fear of other men, much like Alibius does Isabella). This might even act as back-story for the play in that her fiancé's inattention could spur Beatrice on to less repentant sex with De Flores. In Reynolds Alsemero feigns a trip only to hole up in his bedroom with an arsenal of weapons. When the lovers get together immediately Alsemero rushes in on them in bed together, guns them down, and proceeds to hack them to pieces. Reynolds obviously rejoices in this act of 'justice' and the murderer gets off scot-free because of the original sin of murder and adultery by his victims. Middleton again deepens the psychology by having the lovers become the anti-heroes and take their own lives while their accusers limply look on. In *The Changeling* it's hard to feel the same sense of 'God's revenge' as Reynolds righteously summons for his parables' characters (Alsemero is later hanged for killing Tomazo in a duel; God's revenge for having *thought about* murdering Alonzo and for chatting up Beatrice in a church). Middleton treats his audience like grown-ups and reveals a world where the 'evil-doers' can be more sexy and sympathetic than the flaccid and tiresome 'good guys'. The play conjures an adult duality that explodes myths of love and marriage that are treated as prescribed parables for children in Reynolds.

It's a sign of the times that Middleton and Rowley were able to turn a religiously zealous tabloid where fun will kill you into a kinky anti-morality play where the bad seeds go down in a blaze of glory. (As a side note the name of Rowley's character 'Alibius' most likely comes from the story following this one in Reynold's *Triumph*. The plots, however, have nothing in common.)

The second source for the main plot and Middleton's inspiration for the deeper characterization of De Flores is from the novel *Gerardo the Unfortunate Spaniard: or a Pattern for Lascivious Lovers* by Gonzalo de Cespedes y Meneses (March 1622). In a translation by Leonardo Digge, this story provides the lurid inspiration that makes

*The Changeling* a raunchy pot-boiler rather than a religious primer. In *Gerardo* the Spaniard sexually blackmails a soon-to-be bride and a 'wedding night bed trick' must be performed to cover up her lack of virginity. Though this plot device also appears in John Webster's *The White Devil* of 1612, the deception of subbing the virginal Diaphanta for the recently deflowered Beatrice–Johanna would have been fresher in *Gerardo* for Middleton as he completed the play in May of 1622. Rowley also drew from the novel's plot in 1623 for his *The Maid in the Mill.*

Finally, a minor source for this plot is from a treatise by pharmacist/botanist Antonius Mizaldus titled *Centuriae IX Memorabilium*, which includes similar recipes (though not the exact one Beatrice cites from Alsemero's closet) for the detection of pregnancy. Beatrice misnames the book as Mizaldus' *Secrets in Nature* but the reality is that these chemical recipe books were often compilations with room for notes and discoveries by the user. By the seventeenth century traditional alchemy, a pseudo-science concerned with the transformation of elements (most notably lead into gold), had evolved into chemistry. Rejecting some of the mumbo jumbo that blurs the lines between traditional medicines and mythical panaceas, chemistry at the time of the Jacobeans was just starting to strive to produce repeatable results. Despite this growing rejection of the magical, quackery like Alsemero's medical cabinet, filled with chemistry-set concoctions that offered amateur cures and diagnoses, was very much en vogue. Whether the pregnancy test is a silly conceit to further the plot or comes from a chemical combination that Middleton believed existed is unknown.

## Sources: Rowley

*The Changeling*'s comic sub-plot needed no direct source for inspiration since it's the marriage of an ancient joke and a contemporary fad. The joke is the timeless 'farmer's daughter' story of the older, cuckold-worthy husband protecting his young, bird-in-a-cage wife from wily, virile suitors. The husband ends up inviting the fox into his closely guarded henhouse believing the young man is beyond reproach. Surely this story goes back to prehistory, and all of recorded history features versions of this old tale from the Greeks to commedia dell'arte to the modern dirty joke. Every culture, it seems, has a word for a man who unknowingly shares his wife with another (although if it's with his consent he's technically a *wittol*). In Europe the image is most often associated with the horns of a billy goat while in Japan they say he 'wears a green hat'. Ultimately in *The Changeling* the threat of cuckolding of Alibius is treated as a joke whereas when the deed is actually done to Alsemero the results are bloody and horrible. The old joke is actually the set up for *both* plots; it just feels more realistic in the main castle plot and cartoonish in the asylum.

The fad that provides the setting for Rowley's plot is the practice in the seventeenth and eighteenth centuries of visiting asylums for entertainment and employing their inmates as courtly entertainment. A modern stage example of this ignorant cruelty is in Peter Weiss' *The Persecution and Assassination of Jean-Paul Marat as Performed by the Inmates of the Asylum of Charenton Under the Direction of the Marquis de Sade* (1963), which surely benefits from the example of *The Changeling*. In this Marxist-hippie agit-prop, the conceit is that the moneyed owner of the Charenton Asylum makes the ill-advised choice to let de Sade direct a patriotic play about the French Revolution only to witness that anarchy reigns when the mad are in charge.

In his *Bedlam on the Jacobean Stage* (1970: 1) Robert Rentoul Reed described the Jacobean stage as 'a patient in the psychopathic ward running amuck with fever, his brains afire'. Madness and its treatment seem to have never been more in the public interest unless we look at our own current fascination with pathology and forensics. Reed characterizes the Jacobeans as obsessed by 'unusual abnormality, extravagance, and bombastic utterance'. The people wanted to see a 'reckless pace' on stage that reflected England's own, a world where rules were made to be broken. Careening towards civil war and Cromwell's attempted prohibition of immorality, Jacobean London was in a state of psychological crisis where the mad were embraced as fascinating, rather than marginalized as with the 'madwoman in the attic' culture of the Victorians.

In Rowley's madhouse plot Alibius' slapdash asylum was almost assuredly based on London's Bethlehem Hospital or 'Bedlam' as it was popularly known. Dating back to the thirteenth century, the hospital began admitting the mentally ill in the mid-fourteenth century (before then monasteries typically cared for the insane). It featured a 'Keeper' much like the character of Lollio who was paid by families or parish charity for each patient he attended. Disgraceful neglect led inmates to draft a petition to the House of Lords in 1620 demanding better conditions. Although there are almost no eyewitness accounts on what went on in Bedlam during the seventeenth century, Rowley's scenes of asylum life match up with eighteenth-century written testimonials. In fact Jacobean plays often provide the only reportage on asylum conditions and operating practices at the time. Civilians went to Bedlam as a place of curiosity and amusement. For the price of a penny one could gawk at the mad and thousands of spectators each year chose to do so.

In *The Changeling* Alibius' madhouse (called 'bedlam' at one point) is most likely a public one if it was open to civilians. If there were other public asylums in London at the time Bedlam is the only one that appears to have admitted visitors. Guests would likely have witnessed inmates with lesser afflictions like dementia and 'melancholia' (as clinical depression may then have been known). In Bethlehem the mild cases were kept separate from the more severe 'maniacs' in different wings and it may be that the offstage screams heard in *The Changeling* come from the cells of the latter. Weiss' *Marat-Sade* is set in 1808 and features a fascination with the insane that, like the interest of the Jacobeans, flared up again in the 1960s. Similarly *One Flew Over the Cuckoo's Nest* (1975) and *Girl, Interrupted* (1999 but set in the 1960s) continue the ongoing tradition of viewing the mentally ill as a source of alternatively disturbing and funny entertainment.

There is little doubt that conditions in seventeenth-century asylums were brutal. Food was scarce and under-nourishing; cells were unheated and featured only straw for bedding. Crowd control was an issue as patients (the term didn't come into use until the eighteenth century) often protested foul conditions. That a Keeper might indulge his whip hand as Lollio does is not unlikely. Therapy consisted of whipping (a long-accepted cure for dealing with 'devil sickness') and being locked in small, dark spaces. Ironically the modern therapies of restraint, electro-shock and sensory deprivation may in fact just be prettier versions of their ancient predecessors. King Lear is temporarily brought back to sanity by music and pharmaceutical cures were known to exist in the 16th century but Bedlam didn't offer these techniques. It's not beyond possibility that, considering the crude diagnostics of the time, 'changelings' like Antonio and Franciscus could infiltrate Alibius' madhouse as imposters.

Patients at Bedlam were usually only admitted if they were deemed curable and a surprising number were apparently returned to sanity. It's debatable whether Lollio and Alibius are actually working to rehabilitate their charges or simply to force them into submission and keep the money for their 'care' coming in. Alibius' character was probably modelled after the notorious (and with a name straight out of Dickens) Dr Crooke, master of Bethlehem at the time the play was written. Largely an absentee hospital director like Dr Alibius, Crooke also left his Keeper to run the hospital. Both men accepted kickbacks at the expense of their patients' dignity and Crooke exercised his connections with the Court as a provider of entertainment. After an investigation in 1632 Crooke and his lackey were convicted of extortion and dismissed.

Bedlamites are featured in many Jacobean plays including Dekker and Middleton's *The Honest Whore*, Dekker and Webster's *Northward Ho*, Fletcher's *The Pilgrim*, Webster's *The Duchess of Malfi*, Ford's *Lover's Melancholy*, Jonson's *Bartholomew Fair* and alluded to in Shakespeare's *Measure for Measure*. The Jacobeans could not get enough of this fascinating sub-culture, one anyone could end up a member of if the mysteries of sanity give way to madness.

# 4 *Key Performances and Productions*

## Infinite works

Whether it's the artistry of the director, the actors, the designers or the musicians, a stage production's effect is largely a matter of where the 'spotlight' has been focused. The same is true for all works of art; we respond to how the artist accentuates elements like language, colour, humour, rhythm, pathos, imagery, shape and dissonance. Countless tools work together to create a story or to convey a non-narrative experience and no art form is as collaborative as theatre.

A 'conventional' approach to a play like *The Changeling* might feel unaffected and pure – or it could strike us as devoid of ideas and flat. An 'experimental' staging could thrill through bold imagery and interpretation, mining the complex levels of meaning in an archaic text – or it could slam the door in our face if we find it prurient, revolting or lamely art-for-art's sake.

When fully staged for a paying audience, any piece of theatre undergoes countless 'mutations' beyond the conscious choices of its creators. An actor may set out to make a role 'sympathetic' or 'disturbing'; a director might wish to declare a socio-political state-ment; a designer could aim for minimalism or sensual overload; and one musician's sensitive score could strike another as completely inappropriate and alienating. Intention is not the same as reception and it's the audience that completes the circuit begun by the artist.

'Mutations' is a term we might use to describe the elements beyond the artist's control that effect our perception of the work of art. The vocal ability of the actor, the director's religious beliefs, the designer's sense of shape, or the musician's fear of repeating herself might all affect us, positively, negatively, ambivalently, more than any conscious choice these artists laboured over during the creative process. When experiencing art our individuality transforms the 'concrete material' of the work in a uniquely liquid way. As audience members our own preconceptions seize upon both the artists' conscious choices as well as their subliminal impulses, filtering them through our personal worldview. How we feel about infidelity, war, race, justice or gender roles, for example, all deeply colour how we receive the myriad signals and symbols of a work of art. Not only does the artist in the theatre translate a fixed, encrypted source, the script, into a work of infinite possibility; the audience further adapts the adaptation. Even if one remains emotionally neutral, the stimulated mind stirs in a potion of singular memories and responses that create a new work for every spectator.

## From the ashes

*The Changeling* was 'reborn' in 1961 with director Tony Richardson's production at the Royal Court in London. While audiences giggled at the macabre moments, critics were dissatisfied with Mary Ure's Beatrice whom they generally found physically attractive but trapped in doll-like behaviour that never transitioned into depth. Kenneth Tynan deemed Ure 'a meringue miscast as a hamburger' (quoted in Barker and Nicol, 2004, p. 5) and similar criticism was levelled against Emma Piper's Beatrice in Peter Gill's production for Riverside Studios in 1978. Reviewers of both expected a rapacious power and sexuality from Beatrice that they read as inherent in Middleton and Rowley's text. Roberta Barker and David Nicol in their article 'Does Beatrice Have Subtext?' offer an analysis of how this interpretation is actually a perceptual 'mutation' by drama critics that became the accepted standard. The authors argue that because the critics were united in their damning of these early portrayals of Beatrice in the 1960s, subsequent performances were influenced by the immanence of their official perceptions. It's as if natural selection were at work to promote a sexually repressed, conniving version of Beatrice as more advantageous to telling the Machiavellian story as Middleton and Rowley intended it. For Barker and Nicols this led to performances like Diana Quick's Beatrice for the Royal Shakespeare Company (RSC). Also staged in 1978 but on the opposite end of the interpretational spectrum from Piper's Beatrice, Ms. Quick at the Aldwych was fully a child of Freud. Overcoming her initial frigidity, she surrenders to her sleeping erotic demon, including offering her bare breasts as 'a sexual reward' to De Flores. Director Terry Hands staged her doggy-style consummation with her nemesis graphically but in a way ambiguous enough to be interpreted as rape by some critics and as a consensual-but-rough shagging by others. Was this the fruit of Ure's earlier, tamer portrayal of Beatrice being savaged by critics or the independent interpretation of Quick and Hands? Barker and Nicol contend the former and point to the unity of critical disdain for Miranda Richardson in 1988 (National Theatre) and Cheryl Campbell in 1993 (RSC), both of whom were generally taken to task for playing Beatrice as too restrained and subtle (Richardson) or spoiled and girlish (Campbell). Even when they weren't damning, reviewers' belief in the basic 'duplicity' of Beatrice and her love–hate relationship with De Flores was spoken of as a given. The 'mutation' of early perceptions by influential critics had done its work: for better or for worse the Freudian reading of Beatrice and De Flores' complicated relationship became the accepted one even if, as Barker and Nicol contend, it's the most demeaning, simplistic one to hand. A contention to this reasoning might be that while in theory a love–hate interpretation is a weak one, it's what audiences ultimately desire for the main characters rather than a show of consistency and courage.

*The Changeling* is currently a work more studied than seen, akin to the more problematic works of Shakespeare like *Timon of Athens* or *Two Noble Kinsmen*. Looking at five productions of *The Changeling* staged in the United States and Europe over the past two decades, I aim for a balance of high- and low-profile work. These versions are selected to offer contrast in just how far a canonical work of art can 'mutate' from convention to experiment in an effort to tell a classic (albeit neglected) story. While there's not a wealth of 'above ground' productions of *The Changeling* available for analysis in the early twenty-first century, the work that has and is being done with the play is consistently intriguing.

## Theatre for a New Audience, New York City (1997)

Trumpeted as the first major New York production in 30 years, director Robert Woodruff's interpretation of *The Changeling* at The Theater at

St. Clement's Church was a polarizing one. Based on a production that debuted in a small town outside Tel Aviv, Israel, in 1995, this 'acid-trip adaptation' (*New York Times*) was an apt one to fulfil Theatre for a New Audience's mission to 'vitalize' classic plays. The company specializes in 'adventure' and 'visual boldness', both of which might as well be emblazoned at the top of Woodruff's resume. His work is marked by beautiful imagery juxtaposed with savage sordidness in a blending so profound that the lines where attraction and repulsion begin and end are blurred. His use of modern music and dress and a German-influenced, confrontational style make him the most rock'n'roll of American directors on the large stage scene. Woodruff has directed plays from every era of history and his work on ancient Greek and Elizabethan texts is especially fresh and immediate. His quiver of signs and wonders comes from myriad sources like Kabuki, kitsch American television, punk rock and German Expressionism.

First approached by an Israeli actor friend who suggested he direct the play, Woodruff already had some experience with Jacobean tragedy with his *Duchess of Malfi* in 1993 at the American Conservatory Theater in San Francisco. He'd seen *The Changeling* produced at Harvard's American Repertory Theatre in a version directed by Robert Brustein, who had entirely cut out the madhouse subplot. Woodruff thought it was a missed opportunity for any director: 'Why anyone would want to give up the insane asylum is beyond me' (telephone interview, 2010). In his own production, Woodruff strove for a balance between the two plots, tying them together thematically rather than downplaying or entirely excising the comic one.

This *Changeling* opened with a flamenco-danced, musical dumb-show, introducing the characters and setting the atmosphere for a passionately Spanish world of Alicante. The clean chequerboard floor doubled as a seventeenth-century court and an insane asylum. Ten glass boxes, resembling telephone booths/boxes or convenience store refrigerators created the walls of the set as well as serving as everything from padded madhouse cells filled with women to rooms in Vermandero's castle. Alonzo was murdered by De Flores in one of them and his ghost reappeared there covered in blue paint. Woodruff's penchant for the Grand Guignol, the early twentieth-century horror movement in urban France, manifested itself in the invasive gynaecological searches being performed in the madhouse by Lollio and Dr Alibius. Gratuitous to some critics (one of whom interpreted them as forced clitorectomies), the image is in keeping with the parallel sub-plots where threatened men need to cage and extinguish female sexuality. Woodruff underlined the Jacobeans male's paranoia of women's erotic power and their need to imprison female desire.

When Marian Hinkle's Beatrice began her interactions with De Flores (Christopher McCann) she literally vomited with total repulsion. For Woodruff their affair progresses from his lust and her disgust to a mutually locked, committed adult relationship. She grows up, developing her own sexual agency, gravitating towards a 'sour taste' as many adults do. Woodruff suggests that this is not a relationship motivated by love so much as one in which the full heat of a woman's sexual power is allowed to burn briefly before the system extinguishes it. Photos of the production show the lovers clutching one another, often enclosed by 'walls' and 'passages' suggested by stretched restraining straps and ropes. Sensuality in this world has a sense of desperation about it and is often observed by the play's authority figures with disdain.

A major question at the heart of contemporary theatre is: are we listening any more or purely looking? All five of the productions discussed here opt for either a stripped down, text-centric focus or favour instead a bold style and imagery. Are we still able to listen to and absorb poetic text in a manner close to pre-technology Jacobeans? Or are we looking for visual information that more closely resembles what we witness on computer and television screens? Some critics were turned off by this production's manic pace and wild imagery, feeling that it overshadowed the text itself. Others found it 'visually astounding', one excitedly noting 'bloody crotches are everywhere' (Elyse Sommer, *Curtain Up*, 2007). Woodruff maintains that the attention in rehearsal given to language vs. imagery were as equal forces in creating the production and that one was never stressed over the other. It's a testament to the power of this director's vision, however, that most of this production's reviews barely mention the actors, drawn instead to the imagery and ideas he's spinning. Despite the attention paid to the text and relationships in rehearsal, audiences were hooked by the pictures and what they perceived to be the director's ideas. Woodruff's chosen themes (suppression of female power, the glory of the insane, et. al.) became *The Changeling*'s own and audiences were forced to bring their own ideas to bear as they wrestled with them. Woodruff's work is always active and there is no sitting back for a little passive entertainment, hence the strong responses he always elicits.

While McCann's De Flores was praised by some, *New York Times* reviewer Peter Marks deemed the 'under-trained' leads as unable to pull the weight of their roles regardless of the setting and style. He dismissed Hinkle's Beatrice as 'mild and unthreatening'. This is a common complaint levelled at American actors who don't often get to work in this heightened style. Most university-trained actors in the US have some Shakespeare under their belts upon graduation but very few have experienced the taxing blend of spoken verse and psychotic emotion intrinsic to Jacobean revenge tragedies. This often makes for productions where the physical and emotional (less of a stretch for American actors) are more acutely felt than the power of the text itself. Because public speaking, elocution and rhetoric have long ago disappeared from the American public school system, the spoken word has become less and less nuanced. Most actor training in the US is emotion-based or internalized minutely for the camera, both resulting in underdeveloped voices and a lack of experience negotiating challenging texts. Whether it was this phenomenon at work or just the level of the performances, critics generally didn't praise this production for the acting.

While Woodruff's experiments may have failed to endear *The Changeling* to more traditional viewers, it spurred a generation raised on new technology to find its way back to the original play. For some the conflict between anachronistic elements (the costumes were a modern/period hybrid) and heightened verse was unbridgeable; but do younger, hipper audiences have the same problem as long as the verse is strongly delivered? Modern-dress productions of classic plays have become the norm due to budgetary concerns and the will of directors to tell their 'version' of old stories. Robert Woodruff's love-it-or-hate-it production of *The Changeling* used deliberately provocative imagery, music and ideas to retell an old tale in a style he found fitting for this kinky, passionate play.

## Quantum Theatre, Pittsburgh, Pennsylvania (2005)

In another example of a production transplanted from a distant debut location, Dan Jemmett was asked by artistic director Karla Boos to re-create his stripped-down version of the play in the working-class neighbourhood of Lawrenceville in Pittsburgh, Pennsylvania. Titled *Dog Face* (from a reference in the text to De Flores), the production debuted with French actors in Paris in 2003 at Théâtre de la Ville. The adaptation is basically the entire 'castle' plot with no remnants of the 'madhouse' story intact. Some cuts and liberties were taken as the piece developed but the lion's share of Middleton's verse remained.

Jemmett, is a British national based in Paris who works in Europe and the US and was, at the time of *Dog Face*, married to Irina Brook, the noted director and daughter of Peter Brook. While not as renowned in the US as Woodruff, Jemmett is easily as cutting edged and icono-clastic. His work in Paris included deconstructed adaptations of Shakespeare's *Hamlet* and *Twelfth Night*, and Alfred Jarry's *Ubu*, and he was the first British director to work at the Comédie Française. Much of his work is created through group improvisations and then refined through rigorous physical rehearsals. He doesn't shy away from popular culture sources as influences and was inspired to stage *Dog Face* with a country and western score (some songs performed by the actors, others played from an onstage juke box). Jemmett says the inspiration for adding atypical music to *The Changeling* came from his memory of a relationship break-up he experienced as a young man of 20. Sitting alone, weeping with a bottle of Old Granddad, listening to the music of George Jones, Jemmett knew the episode was both absurdly kitschy and yet had a weighty substance of truth in the moment. He calls it 'real, but induced, melodrama' (personal inter-view, 2010), and hit upon it as an ideal atmosphere for summoning the over-the-top sensibility of Jacobean revenge tragedy (a genre not unfamiliar to him: while studying at the University of London he had read Webster and Ford and felt a strong affinity for these plays, but it was not until he came to Paris that he was driven to direct Middleton's *Women Beware Women*).

When Jemmett decided to rework *The Changeling* he didn't like the subplot, feeling it was merely there because Rowley wrote in a part for himself to play (Jemmett thinks it was Dr Alibius, not Antonio or Lollio). Also disenchanted with what he felt was the more archaic language of the madhouse plot, Jemmett cut it entirely. He preferred to work with the 'shocking and modern' Middleton text on its own, especially in the character of De Flores who he sees as 'up there with Richard III'. He also didn't want a three-hour production like Woodruff's and the Quantum production came in at about 95 minutes.

The frame for *Dog Face* is a band of hard-bitten travelling players, a recurring device in Jemmett's work. He remembers the touring companies of his childhood and spent his young life in art as a street puppeteer. He has a deep fascination for the people who live a 'marginalized existence', inhabiting fairgrounds and side stalls ('carnies' in the US). His love of circus life is one filled with admiration for its denizens even when the attractions are tawdry and underwhelming. The showmanship of Western theatre is about the lives of the performers as much as (or more) than the characters in the texts he selects. He looks behind the curtain at the lurid underbelly of the entertainers who bring us showy spectacle and then limp off to their weathered tents and caravans. This is also part of the attraction in bringing his work to unique locations full of ghosts. In Pittsburgh he staged Michael Ondaatje's book of poetry *The Collected Works of Billy the Kid* with Quantum Theatre in a former porn cinema so haunted and sinister that ritual 'exorcisms' were required before the performances. The dark energy of the sex workers of the space's past mingled with the haunting story created by the actors working in the present.

Quantum performs the majority of its work in environmental or site-specific locations like factories, carriage houses, cemeteries and the Pittsburgh Zoo. *Dog Face* took place in The Heppenstall Plant that formerly produced an array of steel products during Pittsburgh's industrial heyday. Closed since the 1970s, the building lurks on the outskirts of the city's downtown, one of many sleeping giants in a town where the main industry, steel, dried up (though not as irreparably as in automobile-haunted Detroit). Frigid temperatures are the norm for February in Pittsburgh so Quantum suspended radiant heaters that warmed surfaces rather than the air (it would have been impossible in the enormous, draughty space). A mechanical crane, like a frozen dinosaur loomed in the background, framing a circle of sawdust, a trailer/caravan, jukebox and string of lights. This setting felt like a circus, carnival or revival site abandoned by patrons with only the carnies remaining.

Does shifting the 'traditional' location, putting it in modern dress, adding American country music, and changing the name of the piece make it a 'new' play? Ultimately one would have to be familiar with Middleton's *The Changeling* to discern whether *Dog Face* is a strong retelling or its own suggested work. The original play had undergone a series of 'mutations' while keeping one plot and its characters intact, becoming a fresh hybrid – a majority of American audience members, having never read Middleton, would be unable to bring their own experience with the text to bear while watching this production.

The performance began with actors stalking down to the edge of the sawdust-strewn stage and staring down the audience. Alonzo is the only innocent in the piece, with the rest of the cast like a hardened band of carnies that have seen it all. Without any verbal exposition it's unclear as to whether these roustabouts are telling Middleton's story or actually living it. This may be a story they re-enact every night, setting up their tent in a new town, and giving a paying audience a dose of tragedy. Or the carnies might be living this out in 'reality' and their show will never go on due to the carnage that happens this one night. In either case the eroticism of the text becomes purely brutal (Christopher Rawson of the *Pittsburgh Post-Gazette* called it 'more rutting than romance'). Jemmett's take on Beatrice is that she's conniving from the start and that her ruthlessness is the hook that draws De Flores' fatal attraction. This is decidedly not a love story. It's a battle of sexual power and manipulation that Jemmett sees as a sign of the times Middleton wrote in: 'Nothing wholesome, it's all fucked from the beginning' (personal interview, 2010).

John Fitzgerald Jay, a Canadian actor and frequent Jemmett collaborator, played De Flores as a 'driven beast' initially obscured and softened by his 'neurotic array of awkward tics' (*Post-Gazette*). One of the most intense moments of the show was when Jay stepped out of an onstage shower unit and the radiant heating caused steam to boil off of his skin. While the audience shivered, Jay later said it was literally a hot moment for him onstage. Not only diabolical in effect, the image was also one of a baby being born. The dichotomy of wholesome and satanic imagery gave an essence of vulnerability to De Flores' more apparent evil. His (former) work as a street puppeteer made him familiar with attention-grabbing Machiavellian characters like Mr Punch and other archetypal tricksters, and so for Jemmett De Flores is a man of action. Jemmett's fascination with De Flores is his connection to a tradition of villains like Richard III who are 'no bullshit' straight talkers. He thinks Middleton was attracted to Richard's unlikely wooing of Lady Anne as a template for De Flores' suicide mission of bedding Beatrice. Like Richard, De Flores is deformed and loathed and it's his awareness of this shame that makes him ironically sympathetic. We can be swayed to wish both men success even though they are murderers and quasi-rapists. In Jay's charismatic, periodically sensitive portrayal in *Dog Face*, De Flores becomes human and worthy of our understanding. Jemmett calls these villains 'indestructible and fun', bringing a pure entertainment factor and showmanship to the game.

Sheila McKenna played Vermandero in drag with a sleazy country singer's jacket, pencil moustache and pompadour. She wrote original lyrics to a Lefty Frizzell song and sang during Alonzo's ghost's appearance (Laurie Klatscher played the dual male roles of the de Piracquo brothers as well as Diaphanta). The country and western score included 'Folsom Prison Blues' (Johnny Cash), 'Your Cheatin' Heart' (Hank Williams), 'Why Me, Lord?' (Kris Kristofferson), 'Precious Lord' (Carter Family) and 'Honky Tonk Angel' (Dolly Parton). Much like the film scores favoured by modern 'noir' directors like Martin Scorsese, Quentin Tarantino and David Lynch, these well-known songs were used ironically to heighten the tension in the moments they accompanied. Whether to punch up the melodrama in erotic exchanges between Beatrice and De Flores or to bring the English murder ballad (the root of much American country music) back home to roost, Jemmett used music to ratchet up the tension in key moments. Note that the experience of hearing these songs would be radically different for a European audience member than for an American. Even the division between the Northern and Southern states would change the effect of what Jemmett intended to feel kitschy-but-true. What played as ironic in Pittsburgh, PA, might be deemed blasphemous a few hours away in Memphis, TN, where the 'mutations' of audience experience would be wildly different and artists like Cash, Williams and Parton no laughing matter.

Quantum Theatre's *Dog Face* was ultimately most unique as a savage, colourful co-opting of the Middleton plot into a work that felt new and fresh. In what could have been a gimmick full of cheap laughs at the expense of Middleton's tragedy, Jemmett allowed the revenge tale to adapt into a modern noir, maintaining the nightmare and accentuating the brutality of hardened hearts in love.

## Cheek By Jowl, London & On Tour (2006)

Cheek By Jowl is one of the premier touring companies in the world. Formed in 1981 by director Declan Donnellan and designer Nick Ormerod, Cheek By Jowl is renowned for tightly wrought, minutely thought-out productions. Donnellan wrote the popular acting text *The Actor and the Target*, in which he states and restates the need for clarity of stakes in playing a role. This obsessive demand for cutting anything extraneous to the role gives the company its trademark clean, clear style of storytelling. Donnellan and Ormerod are notorious for constantly making changes in rehearsals and asking questions during the run of a production, underlining ongoing important issues so that the stakes remain high and the work never becomes too comfortable and repetitive for the actor. Their *Changeling* reflected this commitment to playing without embellishment.

In this modern-dress production, Donnellan underplayed the pageantry of the court in order to create a spare severity and swift pace. His major licence was to double cast the actors in roles in both of the plots, thereby juxtaposing their themes and obscuring their individuality. The court is literally a madhouse and the asylum a place of social hierarchy and abnormal 'norms'. Donnellan told his cast at the first rehearsal that the deeper aspects of the play moved him more than the bitter external elements of Jacobean revenge tragedy. He underlined the loneliness of the characters, their desires and their ultimate loss. A key theme was the repercussions when one doesn't get what one badly wants. This is a play 'where people talk too much' (website interview, 2006) because they need to justify themselves and their dark desires. He acknowledged his attraction for the modern, film noir feel and sense of psychology in *The Changeling*, siding with those who believe Beatrice acts though a 'hidden attraction' for De Flores. But Donnellan makes a distinction between the character who 'is evil' versus one that 'does something that is evil'. He considers Beatrice and De Flores as belonging to the second group and therefore worthy of audience sympathy. 'We become intimate with these people' and this creates a conflict beyond 'apportioning blame' in a black and white world. We are forced to examine our sympathies if we find ourselves feeling for someone who does something evil. For Donnellan this is asking the audience to think with 'maturity' rather than purely feel from a sense of easy morality.

'It's not for me to get in the way. Absolutely it's for me to be a vessel through which things pass' is Donnellan's philosophy on directing, matching his purist technique of acting in *The Actor and the Target*. He 'tries to vanish' and be 'open to a variety of meanings', qualities he associated with great writers like Shakespeare, Chekhov and Middleton. It's through 'detachment', not rigid ideas, that the artist makes something true. They might have great passion for 'the actions of a character' but there's no 'sentimental blurred boundary' with the characters themselves. Cheek By Jowl's guiding principle is to express the 'immediate visceral sense' of the story but with a 'warm detachment' so an audience can still discern for themselves what that story means: 'That double action is destroyed by acts that are sentimental where you say "This character's good" or "This character's bad"' (website interview, 2006).

Donnellan strives to limit the number of 'mutations' that the director and actors bring to the art, feeling they actually limit the audience's experience and ability to decide for themselves what the play means. The company began rehearsals for *The Changeling* with movement exercises using themes of madness and the relationships between men and women. They added the verse later and then brought it together with the movement, with Ormerod making design sketches based on what he witnessed. Unlike most theatre companies where the designers present the finished designs at the first rehearsal, Cheek By Jowl works in a more organic way, allowing the design to grow as the actors and director develop 'a discipline and a set of rules' during the process of rehearsal. Donnellan calls it 'osmotic' and while it can result in failure it more often makes for ultimate exploration. So while the lack of flashy imagery and shock value may make a Cheek By Jowl production seem less 'experimental' than the work of other companies, the development of the play itself is the ultimate experiment. The difference may be in the group's insistence on truth in storytelling rather than over-the-top images and spectacle.

In the end Ormerod's setting in the London Barbican production was described by the *Telegraph* as 'a bare, dark, cavernous space, ideal for nightmares' (Dominic Cavendish, 8 May 2006). The backstage was visible, though 'carved up by Judith Greenwood's extraordinary lighting' (Michael Billington, *Guardian*, 16 May 2006) which featured many small spots on actors until a fully lit stage at the end delivered a jarring contrast. Only red chairs were used as set pieces, except for a small night watchman's office. The *Metro* describes the effect as one of 'intimacy and expanse' (Claire Alfree, 2006). The production on tour had to perform in every imaginable size of space and the blocking changed radically based on the stages they played.

Will Keen's De Flores had bumpy lesions on his face (the *Guardian* said he was 'just in need of pimple-aid'). Initially daunted by the 'ugliness problem', Keen let that conundrum go and as the tour progressed his view of how to play the role evolved. At first Keen felt he had fallen into 'bad acting' or 'playing the *problem*' ('Olivia Williams, Tom Hiddleston and Will Keen Talk about Their Roles in the Changeling', podcast, 31 July 2006). This means that the actor starts with something that can't change (e.g. 'I have cancer' or in De Flores' case: 'I hate myself'). As the run went on Keen was able to relaxed into 'playing the *solution*' or aiming for the resolution (e.g. making Beatrice become De Flores' lover). This is a more active way of playing the role. Rather than getting mired in impossibilities it becomes all about seeking the possible and, according to Donnellan's method of teaching, identifying a *target* of the highest possible stakes. Keen's De Flores became wittier as he embraced this way of thinking and he felt the character could then enjoy himself in a more natural way, finding glee in his actions. It follows that the actor then finds the 'grace notes' in a role where the character is constantly changing and awakening to new potential. At first Keen had a lot of tension in his hands and arms that became a 'crutch' for playing De Flores' 'buttoned-up' repression. Cheek By Jowl's physical coach told him to release this gesture and find a sense of grace for De Flores but it was difficult for Keen to let it go. He eventually found a much more interesting De Flores with a relaxed body housing a twisted psyche. Donnellan imagined a De Flores with a kind of beauty about him and Keen, by the end of the long touring period, made the revelation that 'someone who hates himself that much actually completely adores himself'. This underlined the sense of the 'antithetical' in the role and gave Keen a wider palette to play within than a one-note 'De Flores is repressed' interpretation. The *Sunday Telegraph*, who saw an early performance, described Keen's De Flores as 'tight-lipped and tight-suited' with 'the fierce sexual desire of a nervous, needy man'. The *Guardian* enjoyed Keen's 'slippery' De Flores and his progression from 'sinister' to 'rather sexy'. His movement was smooth ('he glides and gloats'). The *Metro* called his character a 'pragmatic sadist' and 'an indulgent fantasist', enjoying with 'mechanical relish' the finger-removal scene. Olivia Williams, who played Beatrice-Joanna, has worked primarily in feature films like *Rushmore* and *Emma* as well as on English television. She speaks in a podcast about the actor's (especially the film actor's) need to create a pattern for performing a role ('Interview with Olivia Williams', 8 March 2006). She describes how Donnellan and Ormerod showed up periodically along the tour stops with a virtual 'large removal van' to un-clutter the actors' performances. Williams attests that since she's so often forced to play it 'small' for film that she finds herself playing it 'big' on stage. The *Telegraph* found her to be 'an imperious, fastidious virgin, a changeling of femininity who dabbles in lust and murder', while the *Observer* felt she came on too strong and was unable to make a major shift for her moral downfall (Susannah Clapp, 21 May 2006). These disparate interpretations might reveal Williams' attempts to pull her Beatrice back on the night the *Sunday Times* (John Peter, 21 May 2006) saw her, while giving in to her impulses as a 'frenzied neurotic' on the night the *Guardian* (16 May 2006) was there. When reviews vary so widely as this it can be a sign that a company allows for its actors to experiment and change their performances as the run progresses. Rather than cementing an interpretation the work is ongoing and organically morphing from night to night. The mission of Cheek By Jowl attests to this kind of process-over-product style of making plays and may explain the contrasting reviews.

Tom Hiddleston (Alsemero) speaks in a website podcast of the company's idea that the play begins for Alsemero as a Romeo and Juliet romance between he and Beatrice but is derailed by the murder of Alonzo. After that point he is a 'pawn in the chess game that Beatrice-Joanna and De Flores are playing'. His asides to the audience are made with the assumption that they only know as much as he does, when in fact they've seen it all unfold. He only wakes up to the fact that it's not a play about him when he sees the furtive lovers together. Hiddleston describes Alsemero's tragedy as rooted in his narcissism. He imagines himself to be the main character only to learn he's just a tool.

Hiddleston's idea of the 'blind' aside is a strong guide for the actor playing in a Jacobean play, echoing Stanislavsky's theory that the actor must 'turn his back' on the ensuing events and always play the present moment. If Alsemero strongly expects he's going to win Beatrice's heart then the actor sets him up for a series of blindsides that hit all the harder the more they are in conflict with his expectations. The same is true for the audience. If we assume that the two characters that flirt at the beginning of the play will be the couple in focus throughout, we're blind-sided by the ascendancy of an unprepossessing servant who takes on the role of the romantic hero (or anti-hero).

## English Touring Theatre and Nottingham Playhouse, London and UK tour (2007)

Alfred Hickling of the *Guardian* (4 October 2007) wrote, '*The Changeling* leaves you feeling sticky and ashamed, but Unwin's production is a guilty pleasure nonetheless'.

The director of English Touring Theatre (ETT), Stephen Unwin, formed the company to create a more 'serious quality touring theatre' in the UK and proclaims *The Changeling* to be the 'greatest tragedy in English after Shakespeare' (Steve Orme, *British Theatre Guide*, 2007). ETT produces classical and contemporary work for larger-sized venues and so it tends to be less aggressively experimental in an effort to appeal to a wide variety of audience members. Unwin used elements of period dress and relied heavily on the verse as his 'best friend' for the most traditional of the five productions analysed here. Counter to Robert Woodruff's penchant for graphic, shocking images, Unwin was wary of the play's sex and violence, fearing they might turn audiences off if they were overdone. His madhouse scenes were played for humour and his madmen were unnerving in their dance preparations rather than horrifyingly undergoing treatment/torture. There was an atmosphere that unspeakable things were happening offstage while nothing explicit was actually shown (although the website image for the production is an arresting photograph of a bleeding, gutted Beatrice and dying De Flores). This is a choice where a production of *The Changeling* can mirror the offstage sex and violence of the ancient Greeks rather than that of modern cinema where one can see it all.

Reading professional and amateur reviews of this production one sees the trepidation with which many spectators approach revenge tragedy. They often begin with disclaimers that, although bloody and foul, this production transcended the purely sordid and Unwin is praised for his 'restraint'. One viewer mentioned the play as 'more accessible' than Shakespeare though without skimping on the poetry and depth (Geoffrey Coombe, 'Your Reviews', www.ett. org). These comments reveal much about the way audiences are braced to view Jacobean plays. There's a predisposition to expect gratuitous violence and over-the-top action devoid of beautiful writing or deep ideas. Unwin, fearing the alienation of an audience ready for a gore-fest, steered away from the kind of imagery that Woodruff and Jemmett revelled in. The nature of a UK tour also dictates that what plays as 'gritty fun' or 'real world naturalism' in London might be too much for the smaller towns to which ETT tours. The same is true of any country, attested by the number of musicals and educational plays (which *The Changeling* could be marketed as in Britain; less probably in the US) that tour to provincial communities.

Paul Wills' oppressive set was two levels of grey, dank stone, uniting the plots by representing both castle and madhouse. An exit sign over the metal door ambiguously begged the question of whether one can escape the magnetic forces of lust and obsession. Both castle and asylum contain the sexualities of the young women within them so having one door was apt.

Adrian Schiller's De Flores was described by *British Theatre Guide*'s Steve Orme as 'matter-of-fact' in his villainy, blithely cutting Alonzo's finger off to gain the ring as a love souvenir for Beatrice. The *Stage* called him 'cold and bloodless' and said 'it is hard to put a finger on just what is so unsavoury about him' (we'll excuse the pun). By underplaying his De Flores Schiller attained maximum creep factor without a need for histrionics and his performance was unanimously praised. One viewer found sympathy for him in that this De Flores was 'haunted by disappointment'.

Unwin chose 21-year-old newcomer Anna Koval to play Beatrice based on her youth and sex appeal. For him sex is the bringer of chaos and the actor portraying Beatrice needs to embody that dangerous force. Reviews called her 'highly articulate' and 'beautifully nuanced' (Anne Morley-Priestman, *Whatsonstage.com*, 17 October 2007) and her relationship with De Flores was played as a journey that takes her from repulsion to admiration. Koval's Beatrice was critically hailed as strong, smart and sympathetic while still able to bring out a restless and naive quality. Her scarlet and black lace costume in the first scene reminded one viewer of 'an upper class Carmen in the making'. She ironically exchanges it for a white dress, for the final murder suicide, in Mark Bouman's design. Of course the liberal amount of blood at the end was better showcased in white.

Critics praised the enthusiasm and energy of the ETT cast and their ability to render the text with clarity and immediacy. Ashworth of the *Stage* deemed the production 'riveting' and able to rise above 'mere theatricality', a criticism that tends to haunt the more experimental productions of this play. When reviewers focus on the work of the actors it's often in inverse proportion to the director and designer's injection of bold imagery and other strong stylistic choices. The reviews for the Theatre for a New Audience and Quantum Theatre productions devote a majority of their ink to the world created by their directors and designers with little analysis of the work of the performers. A cliché about theatre-going is 'I didn't like the play but I *loved* the set!' It might not be to the detraction of the productions staged by Woodruff and Jemmet but they garnered most of the glory or the criticism while the actors were largely neglected. With ETT's production it was the lead actors, rather than the director, who attracted the most attention.

## Caffeine Theatre, Chicago, Illinois (2009)

Giving special focus to the roles of poetry and the artist in society, Caffeine Theatre was created by young postgraduates in 2003. The group's 'language-intense, idea-driven' aesthetic led artistic director Jennifer Shook to choose to produce *The Changeling* and another play, *Tallgrass Gothic*, in repertory. Written by Melanie Marnich, *Tallgrass Gothic* premiered in Louisville, Kentucky, at the 1999 Humana Play Festival and is a very loose adaptation of the main plot of *The Changeling*. *Tallgrass Gothic* sets the story somewhere in the Great Plains region of the US, focusing on the love affair between Laura (Beatrice) and Daniel (Alsemero) with the De Flores figure (Filene) much diminished in importance. The characters speak in terse bursts that are alternately brutal and erotic. The Alonzo character (Tin) is actually married to Laura in *Tallgrass Gothic* and is an unlovable swine who we're glad to see vanish. The Diaphanta figure (Mary) is more fleshed out that her Middleton counterpart and adds to the plot's tension as it's revealed she is in love with Laura. The script originally maintained the names of Middleton's characters but Marnich's revised, published script dispenses with all of *The Changeling*'s names. Caffeine chose to present both plays together in order to examine the connections between modern and classical poetic works.

Rachel Walshe, the director of *The Changeling*, focused on the clash between generations and the rebellion of the young. Originally she wanted to dispense with the madhouse subplot entirely (as *Tallgrass Gothic* does) but was talked into keeping a cut version intact. The role of Pedro was removed entirely and Antonio shows up with a note pinned to him, making him a foundling as well as a changeling. Walshe also intercut madhouse scenes in Act III with De Flores' and Alonzo's tour of the castle and prelude to the murder (the same choice is made in Marcus Thompson's feature film version). The production was in the actor-driven category, involving no bold imagery but a heightened tone was maintained by the delivery of the text. Staged on a simple, two-level stage with only buttressed columns to break up the space, the focus was squarely on the intensity of the erotic relationships between the play's lovers.

Shook directed *Tallgrass Gothic* and was inspired by the work of Flannery O'Connor, whose short stories and novel *Wise Blood* are classics of dark American gothic. Mary Shen Barnidge in the *Windy City Times* dubbed it a 'rural-noir shocker'. Amanda Powell played Beatrice/Laura in the pair of plays and her performance in both was described by Shook as an 'iconic, sexy-but-doesn't-seem-to-know-it young woman ... very dangerous to the men around her' (interview, June 2010). She eventually awakes to a sense of agency and her own power.

Jeremy van Meter played De Flores/Filene and was turned on by the challenge of the contrary motives of the two roles. While De Flores is driven by love, his Filene is purely lust obsessed, seeking to drag everyone down with him rather than rooted in any desire to form a partnership with Laura. *Tallgrass Gothic* forgoes the subtlety and cloak and dagger screw-turning that characterizes *The Changeling*, opting for a more cinematic style of erotic poetry (much the same can be said for Canadian playwright Brad Fraser's 1992 adaptation, *The Ugly Man*). The sex is all seen on stage rather than looked forward to (as with the Alsemero/Beatrice scene) or occurring offstage (as with De Flores/Beatrice). In van Meter's imagined back-story, Filene has a history of abuse and the need to gain control in a society where he is powerless. Both ideas work for an analysis of De Flores but in *The Changeling* van Meter ascribed his motives as coming from a place of love rather than damaged inadequacy. He played the part not as 'evil' but as a man who feels honoured to be in Beatrice's presence and willing to kill for her desires, going so far as to call him 'chivalric'. His Filene, however, is simply a 'bad guy' who gets what he wants after bedding Laura on the floor of a barn. Filene's lack of depth and aspiration in *Tallgrass Gothic* reflects Marnich's dead-souled prairie community that is a spare, brutish world brightened only by the early erotic encounters between Laura and Daniel. Any bliss is soon soured by Daniel's frustration at Laura's inability to leave the abusive Tin. It's van Meter's view that both Beatrice and Laura don't see it coming when De Flores/Filene comes to collect for the deed of murder (e-mail interview, July 2010).

Amanda Powell, when asked about what motivates Beatrice, feels that initially she 'found joy in conflict and chaos. I do think this changes – after she stirs things up I think she finds love which binds her to her choices'. Beatrice evolves from bored house cat to fervent woman in love, a deepening that allows her to evolve from a 'petty crush' on Alsemero to an 'intense raw connection' to De Flores equalled by her initial loathing for him (e-mail interview, July 2011).

The setting for both plays running in repertory required the same configuration so designer Diane Fairchild created a simple stage picture that evoked both church and barn. Lighting by Casey Diers sculpted the architecture of the multiple locations. Sound designer Thomas Dixon used heartbeats and string-arranged pop cover songs by Vitamin String Quartet in *The Changeling* and thunder and crows for *Tallgrass Gothic*. Costumes by Richie Fine used period shape with anachronistic highlights for *The Changeling* and plenty of flannel and denim for *Tallgrass Gothic* (the characters could easily be from a production of *The Grapes of Wrath*). Several crossover props were used to link both productions. The dagger used to kill Alonzo/Tin is the same in both and Beatrice's wedding bouquet from *The Changeling* was carried by a ghost at the beginning of *Tallgrass Gothic*. A Spanish-styled, wooden box carved with roses housed the severed finger delivered as a love token by De Flores/Filene.

*Tallgrass Gothic* is in modern prose and feels more cinematic than *The Changeling* but it lacks the depth and intrigue of its source material. *Time Out Chicago*'s John Beer found the double bill created a nice juxtaposition: 'the twin productions offer an intriguing case study in the significance of theatrical style, as the same story gets refracted through strikingly different dramatic idioms'. He describes Walshe's staging as 'straightforward' and 'Elizabethan' and while he liked van Meter's obsessed De Flores he found Powell's Beatrice anachronistic, preferring her 'nebulous erotic hunger in bored farmwife Laura' in *Tallgrass Gothic*. Beer also objected to the 'languid tempo' of Walshe's *Changeling* but praised the 'jaggedly poetic' and 'deeply creepy' *Tallgrass Gothic* text. The *Windy City Times* praised the choice to present both plays in repertory but lamented the 'fresh out of the classroom' inexperience of the young cast with the heightened text and, while singling out van Meter for his 'deft phrasing' as De Flores, felt the cast as a whole fared better with *Tallgrass Gothic*'s modern text than *Changeling*'s verse. Powell agrees, believing the latter's lack of success to be the result of the group becoming 'overwhelmed and confused by the play ... nobody was on the same page ... focusing on different aspects'. While she feels *The Changeling* is a 'complex and thrilling script', she was less excited about *Tallgrass Gothic*'s aridity. The modern play 'is largely based on abstraction and boredom and it is difficult to do, because as an actor, you must make it about something else' in order to make the 'silence, emptiness, indecisiveness, and sadness' active. Still, this familiar, filmic sense made *Tallgrass Gothic* the more popular of the two productions in Chicago where gritty contemporary drama tends to trump classical theatre.

Again the conundrum arises of casting actors young and sexy enough to inhabit the roles of lovers behaving badly while also requiring them to do heavy lifting with the verse text (in the castle plot) or archaic jokes and references (in the asylum plot). That Caffeine Theatre was bold enough to stage an experiment by juxtaposing the two stories with overlapping casts is a testament to their sense of adventure and independence. The two productions shared a reverence for poetry, whether Jacobean blank verse or modern free form, while the youth of the company punched up the theme of the sex-as-rebellion.

# 5   The Play on Screen

What happens to a play when it's made into a film? Does one just shoot a pre-existing stage version or break away from a theatrical setting entirely and take it to locations and film lots? Close-ups are a part of cinematic language that doesn't have an equivalent on stage. How do they focus or distract from a line of text's meaning? Similarly, filmed voice-overs have largely replaced stage soliloquies and asides. What's the effect of this further intimacy of 'reading a character's mind'? Three hours of play text are often cut down to 90 minutes for the attention span of a film audience and long thoughts are broken into smaller, more digestible sound bites. How does this diminish the poetry and its deeper meanings? Imagery becomes more important as the eye does the work and the ear becomes more attuned to the atmospheric musical underscoring than the text, which is often negligible in popular movies. The works of Shakespeare have been filmed in every known permutation from direct stage tapings to blockbuster studio versions to highly adapted teen versions without a hint of original text. How does one attempt to capture the power and the passion of a work like *The Changeling* on the screen?

There are three filmed versions of the play available, two of them made for BBC television and an independent feature film that never made it into wide release. The three are strongly distinct from one another and illustrate different ways to tell the same story based on choices made by the director, editor and actors. As with the stage performances discussed in the previous chapter, *how* the story is told is similarly open to a wide scope of interpretation and imagery but in film the director has the added ability to focus exactly where the viewer is looking and just what she's hearing. In these three films the distinctions can be drawn along two key lines: how the De Flores/ Beatrice relationship unfolds and how much of the original text is utilized, especially in the form of the madhouse subplot.

The ambiguity of the love affair between De Flores and Beatrice becomes especially critical due to film's more focused ability to spotlight the smallest details of their interactions. The subtlety caught by the camera can often be lost when scaled up for the larger requirements of projecting a performance on stage. Conversely, the heightened language and the stage play's inherent melodrama have to be grappled with when every tiny move is scrutinized in close up. The three directors represented here all chose a different means of steering the De Flores–Beatrice affair.

How the broad and zany madhouse scenes are dealt with on screen is another major production choice. On stage they are often damned as too long and obscure to hold the audience's attention, a factor doubled by cinema audiences' expectation that a story can be told in under two hours. All three directors and/or screenwriters have chosen to cut down the asylum scenes or remove them entirely. What's the net effect in what stays or goes? The same can be said for even minor cuts made to the Middleton text. None of the three films retain all of the main plot text but none of them make the same choices about what made it into the final story. Would a modern tele-vision- or cinema-viewing audience be able to handle three hours of the original play in film form? None of the directors, unlike Kenneth Branagh with his four-hour *Hamlet*, attempted to film the entire text.

The litmus test of whether a piece of art works or not is whether the viewer finds truth in it. No matter how faithful or iconoclastic a version of the story might intend to be, plays and screenplays are not machines with one set of operating instructions. The strong choices made in these three films are an attempt on the part of the makers to solve the problems of telling a tale truthfully and with clarity that all can understand.

## BBC 1974

The first televised film version of *The Changeling* is from the 'Play of the Month' series that ran from 1965 to 1983 and featured works by Shakespeare, Ibsen, John Osborne, Sean O'Casey and Dennis Potter. Directed by Anthony Page, it features two major film stars in their youth: Helen Mirren as Beatrice Johanna and Brian Cox as Alsemero. Unlike the anachronism-embracing stage versions discussed above, the settings and costumes by Fanny Taylor and Betty Aldiss, respectively, are decidedly seventeenth century with extensive attention paid to detail in the weaponry on the walls and even the saddle De Flores cleans in his first meeting with Alonzo.

This version might be best described as a wolf in sheep's clothing. From the opening scenes we are led to believe that this will be a staid, by-the-book affair in the style of many of the BBC's Shakespeare series. While some of those films stand out many can be arid and unadventurous, seemingly designed to alienate school kids from classical theatre. Page's *Changeling* deceptively begins in this vein with an interaction between Mirren's doll-like, simpering Beatrice and Cox's one-note, gloomy Alsemero that almost begs one to stop the disc and watch something else. Stanley Baker's stiff and overly villainous De Flores doesn't relieve the turgidity, adding to the sense that this is a dusty melodrama with a plodding stock plot.

Then something wonderful happens. After this deft use of lulling misdirection Page begins to expose the cracks in the masks of the characters. In the Act II murder scheme the camera reveals the tiny lines in Mirren's face, her Beatrice grows spikier and imperious, shedding her baby-doll looks for quick glimpses of a hardened woman beneath the girlish surface. Her poodle hair, long lashes and thickly painted skin, are in fact hiding her true, darker self beneath a geisha's mask and frilly gowns. Cox's Alsemero, seemingly just a pouting pretty boy, by Act IV is revealed to be a sadistic bastard who never wanted anything more than to own a trophy wife. Baker's De Flores changes least radically but there's something decidedly manly and protective about him in his final scenes. His De Flores is horse-faced and unlovable with an unfortunate haircut but his face is scarred only a by few faint lines that resemble cat scratches. This is surely the least believable 'dog face' make-up of the versions discussed but Baker's creep factor in his early scenes make him far from a good catch. He has an unblinking, surprised look that most often expresses disbelief at the course of unfolding events. It's a unique balance of innocence and the demonic so that when he commits murder it's no shock: his countenance becomes classically cut-throat and reveals it was the sinister side of his duality that reigns. The unblinking stare becomes a remorseless mask as his De Flores transforms after the homicide. Yet he retains a naive optimism for one thing: that having Beatrice for his own will solve all his problems. We start to see past the sharp, Mephistophelean features of the actor and witness the selfless gestures he makes in saving Beatrice. Page and the cast read the text deftly for the 'arc' of the characters and it's the violent change in first impressions that gives this film its punch.

For the murder pact Baker is filled with trepidation. Mirren is bow-lipped and too old to be dressed as a child. Their masks are fully in place as 'Nervous Villain' and 'Damsel in Distress'. Mirren plays the scene sweetly, with a piping voice and winsomeness only a fool would fall for but her hands give away her intentions. Her lips praise De Flores but the spasms of her fingers express her repulsion. In her expression of 'hardness becomes the visage' some glimpses of a dark attraction for De Flores start to emerge and their masks begins to slip. When she wishes she had been formed a man her gambit to excite his interest is clear and cunning. Her anxiety mounts as she negotiates what will happen with De Flores, her strong switches of intention and emotion driving this intricate cat-and-mouse scene forward in a dynamic way. She shouts, 'Dog face!' in a voice-over aside but she looks as if she's just experienced an enormous orgasm. These two scenes are largely Mirren's as Baker plays them mostly flat and as a receptor to her many shifts and switchbacks.

In Act III, scene iv, the moment-to-moment playing captures the electricity of Middleton's text. The actors read the 'blueprints' of the text with a deftness that allows the scene's schizophrenic switches to feel organic and justified. In the first moment Baker returns from the crime like the cat that got the cream, certain of his recompense. Mirren looks as if she's eaten something that's making her sick and briefly weeps at the news of the deed. They are revealed as tears of delight and her bosom heaves with relief and excitement. She is genuinely repulsed at the sight of the gift finger, however, and this begins a downward spiral. When Baker thinks she may be trying to buy him off he darkens and turns threatening. These are all *choices* made by the actors base on their reading into the motivations of their roles. They strive for the most truthful way of conveying what the characters are experiencing but our need for novelty demands that we are constantly surprised by the way things play out. After a moment of fear Mirren's Beatrice girds her loins to stand up to De Flores and brush him away. She manages a strained smile and takes a higher status, making him give ground and doubt his ability to win her affection. What improvisation master Keith Johnstone calls the 'see-saw' of status is in effect here as De Flores' broodingly calls her bluff and she panics, swatting him in an effort to get him to leave but his threats trump her palpable terror. This scene is most certainly a rape and not a seduction. Mirren is wide-eyed with horror and tries to escape as Baker's De Flores becomes increasingly disgusted with her refusal. She weakly threatens him like a petulant child and he clutches her face, hurling her to the ground. She eventually submits to him, kneeling before him in a pose that suggests forced fellatio. Rather than further pushing this brutishness like we'd expect of a remorseless rapist, Baker receives Beatrice's consent with giddy delight and nearly weeps with joy. This 'playing the opposite' deepens the role and earns an uneasy empathy due to the complexity of the man we're dealing with. Rather than being won over Mirren's Beatrice is obviously terrified, rigid and quivering in his enforced kiss.

A major directorial choice here is Anthony Page's decision to accentuate rape as the turning point for Beatrice's subsequent affection/love for De Flores. In 1974 when BBC's *The Changeling* was made the transforming identities of women and the vigorous pursuit of equal rights also brought to light the prevalence of rape and domestic violence in male–female relationships. The twentieth century's shift in the social roles of women as they transitioned from primarily mothers and housewives to a greater part of the workforce were especially reflected in the art of the 1960s and 1970s. The revolution also extended to women's sexuality and how it was portrayed. In 1971 director Sam Peckinpah's film *Straw Dogs* featured a graphic scene where Susan George's young, married character is raped by two local workmen, one a former lover. Much contention arose over whether her character was actually consensual in her own rape or if she was submitting in order to avoid being murdered after the deed. Her husband is a scrawny academic while his assailants are brawny sensualists and so it was posited that she may have invited the excitement of wild, proletariat sex. Accusations of misogyny and rape fetishism were levelled at the film and the controversy kicked up a firestorm that led to the film's censoring in the United States and later banning in England (although it played there in 1971 with an X rating). Also in 1971 Stanley Kubrick's *A Clockwork Orange* spawned similar outrage for its depiction of rape and 'ultra-violence'. This time it was from a young, sociopathic male's perspective and clearly not consensual. Although perceived as social satire by some, the rollicking nature of the rape scenes left others adamant that the abuse of women was being condoned as a joyful affair. The scandal of both films and the rape debate raging at the time were in the air in 1974. They no doubt influenced Page's reading of both De Flores' violence in forcing the terrified Beatrice to submit and her subsequent acceptance as her lover. Like Susan George in *Straw Dogs* one can argue that Beatrice is just bargaining for her life as she gives in to De Flores but her subsequent teaming up with him is then hard to substantiate. If this is simply Stockholm Syndrome then Mirren plays it with a newfound authority and depth for her Beatrice. (The film was made just one month before Patty Hearst, an American newspaper heiress was kidnapped and became a bank robber for the Symbionese Liberation Army, raising similar questions about how far brainwashing changes one's persona.)

After the wedding scene, Cox plays Alsemero as a sweaty drunk and Mirren, upon coming to confront her new husband struts in with a freshly acquired, wanton manner. Though she claims she'll miss the joys of her wedding night one sense that she can take it or leave it since she's no longer a virgin anyway. Her affections are moving towards De Flores and suggest she likes the rough treatment he's inflected upon her. While she appears timorous with her husband she is visibly outraged by the virginity test he administers. Her feigned laughter is in mockery of his pitiful efforts to discover and control her. Later when De Flores arrives while Beatrice is waiting for the bed trick to play out, she clings to him in a desperate effort for a solution. Their relationship has completely changed just like in the classic film scenario where the strong-willed, shrewish heroine finally comes around to needing the ill-mannered, macho hero. Baker transcends his creepiness and proves masculine and direct and they share a blissful kiss. It's clear that now she's fully in love with her former enemy. She sees Alonzo's ghost at prayer, complete with close-up on the severed finger, but when she's alone again the fire bell plunges her back into ecstasy. A lovers' intimacy passes between Beatrice and De Flores as they put the matter of Diaphanta's passing to bed. By Act V, scene iii, Mirren has fully metamorphosed into a slut, unrepentant and brazen. Cox tries to strangle her and she desperately bargains for her life, making herself a pouting victim. It's a scene straight out of a film noir like *Double Indemnity* or *The Postman Always Rings Twice*. When Cox repents, Mirren looks away, obviously dreaming of her lover De Flores. She plays the child again but this time the discrepancy between her prostitute looks and how she play-acts gives her away. Her final speech as she's dying is not at all erotic, delivered with a deeply supported, mature voice and clearly adoring her murderer. Their final tableau together is sensual and tender.

This was an early camera appearance for Mirren and she was learning the ropes as she went. A great admirer of Jacobean tragedy, she says in an interview that she is attracted to these plays' romantic, gothic nature and imagines that if she were a young girl today she'd be a goth so she could express externally the passion she felt at that age. Jacobean women appeal to Mirren as sensual and uninhibited in their impulses, however sinful (*Mirren at the BBC* interview). She praises their dichotomy and complexity and would love to do a modern-day version of *The Changeling*. Specializing in playing sensual femme fatales, Mirren came closest to playing another Beatrice in Peter Greenaway's controversial 'modern Jacobean' love story, *The Cook, the Thief, His Wife, & Her Lover*, which features scenes of sexuality and violence worthy of Middleton. Renowned for her uncompromising performances, it's not surprising that even so early in her career Mirren would interpret Beatrice as driven by her rape to love her rapist. She says she believes Beatrice's great repulsion leads directly to her obsession: because De Flores is from a lower class she can't regard him as an equal but it also draws her uncontrollably to the animal passion he represents. The film itself suggest that Beatrice is a wild horse that, once violently broken, becomes docile to her breaker and utterly devoted to him. While Page and Mirren don't attempt to unequivocally solve the riddle of Beatrice's warming to De Flores they do make the catalyst clear in her attempt to escape her rapist. A strong choice, but not the only one as we'll see with the version that followed 20 years later.

Page plays fast and loose with his madhouse scenes, cutting them up, removing large sections and presenting them in a different order than in the original text. They don't really come to much except as a showcase for an antic madhouse bergomask dance at the end of the sub-plotline. The Act I scene with Pedro and Antonio is moved to the end of Act II where Kenneth Cranham's Antonio is pretty, sweetly vague, and easily excitable to tears. His bantering with Lollio (Norman Rossington) is much cut down, which makes for swift, clear action, unhindered by the play's archaic humour. Lollio and Alibius' deal to keep Isabella (Susan Penhaligon) sequestered from gallants is moved to directly follow this scene. The role of Francisco is entirely cut putting the focus onto only one suitor for Isabella. Rossington's Lollio, while earthy and crude, downplays sexual innuendo to appear the cool, reliable warden to Alibius' charges, including his young wife. As is common in recent productions, madhouse scenes are also used here to break up De Flores and Alonzo's castle tour.

Penhaligon's Isabella is a ringer for a brunette Beatrice but rather than playing the sweet little doll she is all spoiled brat. Lollio is brooding and moody with her, playing up the juxtaposition with De Flores but losing any sense of being a pornographic clown. In fact, these scenes are not played a comic at all; they are all about power and menace. Isabella is strong-willed and petulant and Lollio is fed up with her tart tongue. Page cuts to Antonio's harried love scene with Isabella where his head has been shaved and he is truly desperate to pledge his love. Isabella softens under his onslaught of affection and eventually submits to his kisses while a deeply jealous Lollio looks on. He purposely releases the madmen for a dance rehearsal to break up their rendezvous. With Antonio out of the way the attempted kiss between Lollio and Isabella more resembles a back alley throttling. Again, Page directs this scene as another brutal (attempted) rape rather than what could be played as a wacky chase around the furniture. The times may have precluded treating rape as a light subject, even in a comic sub-plot. This section is much shortened by the interruption of Alibius (Raymond Francis) and Isabella is sharply spiteful with her distracted old husband.

The dress rehearsal of the madmen's wedding dance is truly a joyless phantasmagoria featuring a raucous tarantella. Isabella is clearly disturbed and her would-be lover Antonio is conscripted to play a devil while Alibius is pleased by the progress as Lollio directs by cracking a whip. The scene ends with Antonio being tossed into the air on from a piece of sacking, quoting directly from the work of Goya. This is a hellish landscape devoid of any fun and has the unexpected effect of making the castle plot look like the more hopeful one. While there are some juxtapositions left between the lives of Isabella and Beatrice, Page's cutting and transpositions largely savage any resolution of Isabella' caged-bird storyline. The last time we see her she's a pawn trapped in purgatory rather than a cunning woman who commands what little agency is hers to take. If the subplot exists to illustrate an alternative reality for Beatrice had she been able to overcome her desire to erase Alonzo, it's obscured in Page's truncated telling. Perhaps he's saying that it's better to taste forbidden fruit like Beatrice and burn out brightly than to fade away like the good girl, Isabella; but by giving short shrift to the madhouse plot it ends up feeling like more of a distraction from Beatrice's tale than support of it.

While much of the Middleton text up until Act IV remains with only minor trimming, longer speeches like Beatrice's physician's cabinet monologue are severely cut. Here the re-shaped version gets the job done in a shorter, more pulse-racing manner than the original and would be a good script to crib from for a stage production seeking to maintain a swift pace. When Beatrice administers the chemical virginity test to Frances Tomelty's lusty Diaphanta only the laughing symptom has been named and looked for. Here we can start to feel Page slashing text as he races towards the conclusion. When De Flores and Beatrice are locked in her bedroom we see them and most of Alsemero's lines are cut or muffled, delivered from the other room. Their final moments alone together become more interesting than Alsemero's idle threats and Beatrice's murder is caught on camera. Otherwise, Page's cuts are conservative and sage, allowing the action to gallop forward without losing subtle meaning along the way.

Page makes two other choices that are unique in this film. First, the camera periodically offers close-ups on objects like De Flores' satchel as he deposits Alonzo's finger and the cask that holds his bribe money. Page dwells on these objects before moving ahead. Containment and holding images abound just as Beatrice and Isabella are kept and held in their cages. The small prisons reflect the big ones, all holding their ill-gotten treasures: a dead man's finger and dirty money are traded on the same black market as Beatrice's virginity or Isabella's fidelity. Second, in Act IV, scene i, after a very brief wedding dumb-show there follows a dream sequence featuring members of the cast in white (except Tomazo in black) swirling throughout the castle walls. Beatrice uncovers a small python from a pile of clothing and bloody stairs and a bleeding Beatrice foreshadow the play's end just before she wakes from the dream. One reviewer called this sequence '70's twaddle' but it does give a sense of panache to an otherwise straight-laced production that takes few liberties with imagery. One wonders what the inclusion of more surreal, subconscious-dictated scenes would have done to Page's overall storytelling.

## BBC 1993

The second BBC televised film, produced and directed by Simon Curtis for his long-lived *Performance* series, is an unassuming master-piece. Featuring pitch-perfect performances in all the roles, most surprising is the one by its sole American actor, Elizabeth McGovern, as Beatrice. Curtis' wife, Ms. McGovern was on her way to becoming an A-list film actor in the US in the 1980s, but nothing really prepares one for her astounding Beatrice. Her china-doll looks are the ideal counterpoint to her deep, commanding voice and although she also resembles a toy like Mirren, McGovern doesn't begin as childish or dismissible. Her ability to snarl one line and coo the next belie a visceral understanding of the spoiled-but-trapped bird that is Beatrice. It's a role that confounds a sense of balance in most actresses; either they come across as too forward or too mild, too prudish or too sexual, but McGovern hits all the marks. Rather than displaying a strong shift from doll baby to hardened vixen like Mirren, McGovern plays all the notes side by side in a portrait of spiralling complexity. Her Beatrice is a force to be reckoned with.

Her co-star, Bob Hoskins, while less of a surprise, is equally adept and attacks the role of De Flores with the just the right weight and intensity. The fact that he is about a foot shorter than McGovern underlines both Beatrice's power and De Flores' Napoleon complex. You can feel his desire to drag her down to his level. Hoskins' well-established thug's growl alternates with an inky, trained stage actor's mastery of verse to flesh out his obsessed but controlled De Flores. He sports a half-faced vascular or port-wine birthmark that is disturbing upon first sight but distinctive as you get to know De Flores. It also gives him a red devil's face when shot from the right.

As with Page's 1974 version, the opening scene is played with a stiffness that belies the depth the film attains once it gets rolling. Hugh Grant's Alsemero initially resembles the formal painted back-drops behind him on the 'quay' and the obviously fan-produced wind doesn't do much to sell the setting. But Grant's irritable, aloof Alsemero soon gives way to the blinky, mawkish charm he replicates in countless other roles. The film finds its groove as McGovern and Hoskins develop an indelible passive–aggressive attraction. While her Beatrice plays hard to get with a knowing smirk for Alsemero, she lets De Flores have it with an irritable, hateful delivery. While Mirren went for prissy in Beatrice's revulsion with her father's valet, McGovern is sneering and callous, then able to immediately morph back to being alternately innocent and sultry with Alsemero. When Hoskins receives the glove from Beatrice at end of Act I, he smells it like a dog and then draws it onto his hand, ripping it open in the process. It's both a vengeful violation and an arousing, worshipful manoeuvre that sets up the rape vs. lovemaking ambiguity that Middleton (but not Curtis) leaves us to argue.

In their first heated exchange in Act II McGovern's 'How wise is Alsemero in his friend' speech is darkly psychotic, followed by Hoskins' breathlessly agitated and then disgusted 'Yonder's she' soliloquy. Switching effortlessly into spoiled brat mode, McGovern watches with feline interest as Hoskins can't stay away despite her aspersions. He comes in too close for a near kiss and their mutual expression is one of familiar lovers rather than sparring nemeses. During De Flores 'Garden-bull' aside, McGovern's Beatrice watches him from the background and after his exit fans herself, sexually excited, moved in a way all her A-named suitors could never elicit. In fact, we start to see Beatrice's fading interest in Alsemero in their next meeting. McGovern is condescending and dismissive when he offers to challenge Alonzo to a duel. In her voice over she sinks to a deep, dark witch's growl only to pop out of it with a plucky facade as if all is well. Her black heart is looking more matched to a De Flores than an Alsemero and their attraction is plainly mutual.

The jewel of the play and this film is the scheme to murder Alonzo, set by Curtis in a room that resembles a large confessional with crosshatched windows and flickering candles. After a deeply schizophrenic love scene with Alsemero where McGovern shows her Beatrice to be the ultimate changeable actress, De Flores appears at the window like a priest at a confessional. McGovern morphs effortlessly from breathlessly lying about De Flores' recently improved looks to softness, sensually toying with a candlestick. All the while Hoskins' appears about to swoon and die a happy man. The asides are delivered in voice-over throughout the film and here they are artfully slipped into the conversation, whispering the private thoughts that drive their intentions. Unlike on stage, these asides don't require the push of projection so they feel subliminal and organic. McGovern employs a new tactic, becoming simpering, shyly turning away as she feigns being unable to state her dilemma with 'We shall try you – Oh, my De Flores!' It's both a transparent gambit and an irresistible manoeuvre and Hoskins takes the bait, begging her to state her desire. This makes him vulnerable as he strives to be her hero rather than an overpowering villain out to control her. He kneels to give up status and remove any sense of threat. With his concern, McGovern loses her playacted desperation to sweetly relay that her request is full of 'horror', 'blood and danger'. This 'playing the opposite' of what the text seems to call for (e.g. greater desperation) is what distinguishes McGovern's brilliant performance. Her ability to mask a line's ugly truth with silky elegance has the double ability to obscure its true meaning from De Flores while pointedly driving her remorseless intention home to the audience. She appears shocked at De Flores' breathless devotion (and her own mounting feelings?) and joins him on the floor. Both become thrilled and giggle together like young lovers, the scene ending in a cheek kiss bestowed by McGovern who still retains a modicum of disgust. After her exit De Flores is enraptured, grasping at space, groping the doorframe, slowly pelvic-thrusting the air before triumphantly somersaulting onto his back. Finally he collects himself and gets back to business. This scene has so many switches, twists and turns it should be shown to any advanced acting class as an example of how to break a difficult exchange into vivid bite-sized beats.

The murder of Alonzo is not broken into pieces by mad scenes yet the swiftness of the deed is not jarring or forced. A graphic finger-severing by jack-knife is followed by De Flores tossing the corpse from a window into a moat. When he tells Beatrice of the deed in Act III, scene iii, McGovern almost swoons. Initially repulsed by the proffered finger, McGovern pragmatically assumes De Flores will accept a buy-out for the deed. She flirts with him while offering the money only to be threatened by a disgusted Hoskins. Internally disturbed but outwardly confident, her Beatrice tries an innocence tactic next when De Flores warns her that if he goes down she does too. 'He speaks home' is darkly aware of the quagmire she's in. When they embrace she is a foot taller than him and she is almost bemused by his pitiful efforts to kiss her. Never does McGovern's Beatrice lose her agency and backbone, even when momentarily off balance. She's less a girl and more an imperious queen in disguise. She loses status and is shocked only when De Flores boldly states his interest in taking her virginity. Immediately she gets on her high horse and spits an idle threat at him but this only amuses Hoskins who scoffs at her class distinctions. They are obviously co-conspirators on the same level and his argument mesmerizes her. Hoskins transitions to a soft, romantic tone despite his threat to expose everything. When he makes to draw away McGovern sensually begs him one final time to accept her bribes but she's like a lover who says no while meaning yes. This may be a morally problematic manoeuvre but it's a bold, revealing moment where Beatrice's conniving trumps any fear of being dominated. She is in control even as she is drawn to kiss him. He makes her come to him and the look on her face could be either ecstasy or repulsion as he takes her on the floor in her billowing skirts. Watch this scene with the sound off and the gestures and facial expressions make it purely a love scene. McGovern looks tempted and trying to resist her urges. The 'see-saw' of status in this scene fluctuates even more wildly than in the Mirren/Baker version but everything is rationalized and given a firm foundation.

In the following scene where a search party combs the castle for Alonzo we see Beatrice taking her pleasure on top of De Flores, clearly in control. After a very brief wedding dumb-show Beatrice is in her chamber in a green (not white) wedding dress and is clearly fatigued by all the secret lovemaking. Her discovery of the virginity test is delivered clearly and without a trace of camp. Her charade of innocence with the dull, giggling Diaphanta is believable and cunning. She proves herself as masterful at setting up a gull as De Flores was with Alonzo. She similarly dupes the suspicious Alsemero. By Act V she's become consumed by a throbbing fever dream. McGovern is snarling and sweaty-faced as she waits for Diaphanta to return from Alsemero's bed, yet she and De Flores are able to scheme the maid's demise like a seasoned married couple. By the end of their planning she is adoringly relaxed and they hold hands like comfortable lovers. Hoskins is unafraid of Alonzo's ghost but McGovern is immediately pale and feverish upon seeing it. Yet she is able to switch vividly into a deeply loving reflection on her hero De Flores. She makes it look effortless and it's exactly the schizoid portrayal that a complex Beatrice requires. She and Hoskins share a loving kiss before all hell breaks lose. Playing at agitation with Alsemero, she needs a moment to think up a lie to tell him about Diaphanta's carelessness with fire. She brilliantly feigns being moved and enraged by her maid's death only to steal a coy lover's look at De Flores. When he is left alone at the end of her performance he is clearly baffled by her stunning 'last hit'.

In the final scene Grant is rigid with anger upon learning that the affair is irrefutable. As she sits at a dressing table in a low cut, red bodice and heavily made-up face (shades of Mirren's whore Beatrice, but less ill-used) and false birthmark, McGovern is agitated but tough with her husband's condemnation. Grant's Alsemero can't contend with her parrying and breaks down. She shatters a glass and spits when she informs him she's had to murder for his sake. Grant is repulsed and feels trapped before locking her up. A wary Hoskins undertakes a showdown of nerves with him before decrying Beatrice a whore. The dialogue up to the double murder is rapid fire and Beatrice's 'oh's' from within sound sexual. As the lovers emerge from the chamber Beatrice is wounded in the hip and De Flores sinks to the floor. McGovern adoringly gazes at Hoskins and looks like a lovely broken doll (the reverse of Mirren's arc?). Her bloody hand stokes his face, mirroring the bright red birthmark that mars it. Hoskins gloats and is in a fit of ecstasy before disembowelling himself and dying in Beatrice's lap. McGovern is resigned, unrepentant and smiling as she dies. Grant exhibits a stiff upper lip as he stands by and witnesses the bloody bodies that end in a tableau like a lovers' picnic.

Elizabeth McGovern's 1993 Beatrice is completely opposite to Helen Mirren's in 1974. Twenty years later the advances of the Women's Movement and the excesses of the 'Me Generation' of the Reagan and Thatcher era have made it safe to turn the tables on the De Flores–Beatrice affair. With McGovern's Beatrice it's *her* desire that ultimately rules the relationship, expressed in her literally being on top. Curtis and McGovern present a woman who doesn't need to be broken by being raped in order to reject her smothering father and possessive husband and join a dark lover in creating mayhem. The rape exploration of the 1970s is played out and an era of complex female non-victims follows in the 1980s and 1990s. The gritty films and protest rock that the Vietnam War produced are replaced by colourful, romantic movies and frivolous pop music.

It becomes safe for the escapism of the 1950s again. McGovern's Beatrice owes more to the selfishness and pleasure worship of the 1980s than Mirren's cracked façade mirroring the jagged shellshock of the 1970s. The 1980s and 1990s were also a time of an increased fascination with 'the rich behaving badly'. Prime-time soap operas like *Dallas, Falcon Crest* and *Knot's Landing* excited television audiences with their irredeemable anti-heroes while the whole world became interested in England's royal family due to the dynamic figure of Princess Diana. The fanfare over her storybook wedding was matched only by the scandal provoked by her escape from a loveless marriage by divorce. Curtis' choice to show Beatrice as the agent of her own desire is no more or less powerful or substantiated that Page's focus on her as rape victim, but it is was more palatable for the times and makes one want to cheer her on rather than dry her tears.

This version retains no trace of Rowley's madhouse subplot but it's clear proof that the main plot can stand alone without feeling truncated or rushed when handled with care. At a manageable 90 minutes, the story makes one grasp why the subplot is so often maligned and slashed down or out. Can one invest equally in the plights of both Beatrice *and* Isabella over the course of an evening? The answer may be that in a theatre we tend to be more patient and can accept more plot and dialogue than in a film. There are plenty of three-hour plays and very few films of that length. Otherwise, screenwriter Michael Hastings makes sparing use of cuts in the main plot in order to keep the action swiftly moving forward.

## Middleton's Changeling (1997)

It's a miracle that Marcus Thompson's feature film of *The Changeling* was ever finished. Many disheartening obstacles presented themselves over the seven years that Thompson struggled to finish a final cut, any one of which might have sunk the hopes of a less obsessive director. It's regrettable that the final film never got the visibility and attention its enormous energy and ambition merit. The finished product itself, on the other hand, might be best left to obscurity. Thompson's *Changeling* is a clear case of reach exceeding grasp despite some intriguing casting and ideas.

Marcus Thompson is a British director who had shot many commercials and music videos but his vision for *Middleton's Changeling* (a misleading title since it includes scenes from Rowley's subplot) is not convincingly realized. The best thing about this film is the stunning location work in Alicante, Spain, where the play itself is set. Thompson's adaptation is a ham-fisted one, featuring scraps of original dialogue peppered with contemporary 'translations' of lines where none are required.

It wasn't until two weeks before filming was set to begin that Thompson found his Beatrice. Amanda Ray-King was a young actress working on a Ken Russell film, *Alice in Russialand*, when technicians on that shoot recommended Thompson test her for his *Changeling*. Striking and poised, Ray-King landed the role but her ability to speak the text is severely limited, matched only by the rest of Thompson's callow cast. In Ray-King, though, Thompson found an ally in his fervent struggle to get the film made. She accompanied him throughout Europe in an effort to find funding for the film, both of them sleeping in a van to save money on hotels. She has since appeared in Thompson's new age fantasy, *A Place To Stay*, and the two are now married.

Although it was suggested that Thompson hire Bob Hoskins to reprise his role as De Flores, the director went with a less likely choice. Ian Dury, a New Wave rock icon who achieved cult fame in his 1970s band Ian Dury and the Blockheads, was hired to play the part. Thompson chose him based on his work in small film roles and a few onstage leads including in Jim Cartwright's *Road*. Dury, who died in 2000, was afflicted with childhood polio and brings a staggering gait and withered legs to his hangdog De Flores. Unfortunately his make-up in the role is absurdly overdone. Looking like a cross between a pineapple and a bowl of oatmeal, his make-up for De Flores is a good example of how *not* to solve the 'dog-face conundrum'. Similarly, his East End dialect and flat delivery, while no doubt an asset in roles like Scullery in *Road*, hinder his ability to make what's left of the text sing. Unlike most of the rest of the cast Dury doesn't push or play emotional qualities, but his simple recitation of lines makes his playing of a passionate murderer preposterous.

In a bit of casting that would have a been a coup, Spanish film star Fernando Rey agreed to play Veramandero but died days before shooting was to begin. Having also lost the actor originally tapped to play Alsemero, Thompson and Ray-King found Colm O'Maonlai in a pizza restaurant. He, like Ray-King, is as striking as an underwear model but wooden and one-note in his delivery. One feels that Thompson must have been casting his film like a music video, i.e. for pretty things that wouldn't have to speak. Baz Luhrmann's *Romeo + Juliet* featured similarly untrained-but-gorgeous young actors but he had the budget and the vision to overload the senses and create a diversion from the actors' mawkish speaking of the original text. Unfortunately for Thompson, constant budget constraints during the shoot (at times to the point of forgoing food for the artists) give the film a slapdash feel.

Walking in the footsteps of 1970s and 1980s art-house auteurs like Derek Jarman and Ken Russell, Thompson's film feels less raw and visceral and more collegiate. His choice to create a combination period and punk world is one that might have worked in masterly hands but the film feels like a lamely constructed university or amateur production. The actors look good but the dialogue is turgid and stripped down to just the utilitarian basics. Costume designer Elizabeth Emanuel (of Princess Diana's wedding-dress fame) created period costumes with anachronisms like Beatrice's Chuck Taylor sneakers worn under a seventeenth-century gown. The sense of broken rules is more off-putting than shocking and adds to the sense that no steady hand is guiding this operation.

All of the interactions between Ray-King and Dury are sexless, flat and devoid of any chemistry. Ray-King's Beatrice never evolves beyond a spoiled little rich girl. Thompson opts for the violent rape motif, but one that doesn't lead to affection on Beatrice's part. Unlike Mirren's sexually compelled Beatrice, Ray-King is violated only to go forth and party hard at her wedding. Rather than attempting to reunite with her new husband and wash off the filth of De Flores (an interpretation none of the films investigate) her Beatrice bickers with Alsemero and goes it alone. There are actually three montages of rape in this film, each of them unconvincingly absurd. The final one happens in an out of control carriage that De Flores has leapt onto in order to exact revenge upon an escaping Beatrice (who definitively has *not* fallen for her rapist). Whether in an effort to be experimental or commercial, the sequence does provide some action to what feels like a long series of brooding commercials or emo videos, but it's a pointless addition. We don't care what happens to the erstwhile lovers by this point since they don't need anything from one another anyway.

The retention of the madhouse sequences, much slashed down, is a blessing and a curse. While they feature the most interesting performances by the clownish Billy Connolly (Alibius) and Moya Brady (Isabella), they are also the most half-cocked and under-cooked. Obviously shot without a set, the camera is locked down in one position as extras parade by in a fashion show/Cirque de Soleil free-for-all. The dialogue is almost entirely obscured and choices like escorting Franciscus via motorcycle gang and dressing Isabella in drag are thin and random. These scenes especially seem like they were shot fast, cheap and with no guiding vision.

The text that is retained is cut down to random highlights and modern phrases are slipped in here and there, giving it a jarring, improvised effect as if the actors are forgetting and substituting their lines. A commitment to an entirely modernized script could have worked and since *Middleton's Changeling* is so heavily adapted anyway it might have been a stronger artistic choice.

The film finally wrapped shooting in 1994 but it wasn't until 1996 that the debut was set for a 2 a.m. showing at the Glastonbury Festival in England. The original cut of the film featured a soundtrack of Jimi Hendrix songs and the music festival was on the 25th anniversary of the iconic guitarist's death. Thompson worked around the clock to finish syncing the score to the final cut but the sound failed at the screening. The Hendrix score was later removed when the artist's family overrode a music agent's tacit agreement with Thompson to use the tracks and defer payment. It was another defeat in a long series of troubles that plagued this film including the final insult of a lack of interest and distribution. While *Middleton's Changeling* did get a screening at Cannes in 1997 ('received with both rapture and hostility' according to Thompson's website), the film played in only one cinema in London's West End and after a brief run regionally in the UK it failed to garner an international release. It is currently available on DVD and, undeterred by his harrowing *Changeling* experience, Thompson continues to make films.

If there's a lesson in Thompson's filmed version of a Jacobean text it's that it's not so easy to take a great work for stage and take it so far afield that it loses all the unities that made it great in the first place. The evocative locations and inventive modern design counteract to one another. The text is violated but without the subtlety and wit that gives modern plays their ability to feel poetic without the use of verse. The actors are beautiful but untrained, passionate but undirected, clear but unfocused. What advantage is a close-up when there's nothing happening in an actor's eyes? What happens to the incredible energy of a room of actors playing madmen when it is generalized and vague? Why subject the audience to repeated rape scenes when there is no exploration of the cause or the consequences? These are all dropped balls that Thompson misses in his mad dash to shoot a large-scale film on a small-scale budget.

## Other *Changeling* projects

*Compulsion* is a loose adaptation of the Middleton plot that appeared as a televised drama on the UK's ITV1 in 2009 (and is available on DVD), featuring Ray Winstone (who also produced) as a De Flores-esque character named Don Flowers. The *Daily Telegraph* called it a 'twisted love story about a privileged girl who has only ever been allowed to exist as a construct of other men' (Serena Davies, 'Interview: Ray Winstone and Parminder Nagra on Compulsion', 28 April 2009). The setting is modern-day London where a rich Indian girl, Anjika (Nagra), employs her father's sleazy chauffeur (Flowers) to kill her fiancé by arranged marriage. The adaptation focuses on the sexual vortex of their murder pact and the 'beauty and the beast' nature of their unlikely relationship.

When Anjika tells Flowers that she hates him he replies, 'At least you feel something'. After their first, tender encounter, she's hooked and begins to take the initiative in their highly sexual affair (even going so far as to close her own car door for herself!). The drama is a distillation of one way of playing the original Beatrice/De Flores relationship: she becomes addicted to the forbidden fruit of loving a beast. Again the rape debate came into play as the *Radio Times* found it to be a 'repulsive' rape fantasy, 'every portly middle-aged man's fantasy' ('*Compulsion* is Repulsive Viewing', www.live2.radiotimes.com, 27 April 2009).

In 1973 playwright Sam Shepard wrote his own adaptation of *The Changeling* but it was never filmed. Called *The Bodyguard*, it was commissioned by director Tony Richardson and set in the American

West. The project never gelled, perhaps due to a bad experience Shepard had as a screenwriter for Michelangelo Antonioni's *Zabriskie Point*. The script has never published.

There is a very low-budget filmed version of the play by director Jay Stern. Shot in six days and without the comic subplot, this Victorian-dress version's trailer is viewable on YouTube (www. youtube.com/watch?v=rI6F96SINco).

# 6 Critical Assessments

In 2007 the holy grail of all things Middleton was revealed. *The Complete Works of Thomas Middleton*, edited by Gary Taylor and John Lavagnino, includes all the works of Middleton collected in a single volume for the first time, creating the kind of resource the works Shakespeare have long enjoyed. Along with its companion, *Thomas Middleton and Early Modern Textual Culture*, the massive undertaking works to resurrect the reputation of an undeservedly obscure master. As an overview of Middleton's rich and varied career and the times in which he wrote in, it's unprecedented; however, I'll be focusing on writings before Taylor and Lavagnino's opus, since that source is so conveniently concentrated for anyone who seeks it out.

When taking a look at the scope of criticism of *The Changeling* one begins to notice a line drawn in the sand between those who see this unique work as a morality play owing more to its medieval ancestors and those who find it a visionary departure from the past, a worthy contender with the pre-Freudian psychology of Shakespeare. Just as in *Othello, Macbeth* and *Richard III* where villains eclipse heroes in their depth and complex motivation, some see Middleton and Rowley's anti-heroine, Beatrice, as a rich female role to rival any Shakespeare created.

*The Changeling* begs the question, 'What is the moral path and who, if anyone, follows it?' Traditionally loyalty and love are cardinal traits of the moral person but if that's the case are not De Flores and (ultimately) Beatrice the most moral characters in the play? Is this a morality play or an anti-morality joyride? Is it revisionist to think the Jacobeans thought the same as we do now in our more secular, globally connected society? Since, aside from Pepys, there are no written opinions rendered by contemporaries of Middleton and Rowley as to how the play worked and was received by Jacobean audiences, we are left to do detective work from how the play hits us now. By trying to analyse *The Changeling* in the context of seventeenth-century London, some critics feel closer to understanding how we might interpret it today. Only by combining the past and the present can we make informed decisions on just what this ambiguous story is really trying to tell us.

## Early critics

In 1661 Pepys rendered the first criticism of the play, recording a rave review for a performance of *The Changeling* in his infamous diaries with the terse note 'it takes exceedingly'. Nineteenth- and early twentieth-century critics, unable to see an actual professional production of the play, are split in their reactions to the merits of the anti-hero leading roles.

In 'The Plays of Thomas Middleton' (1843), James Russell Lowell, although a pre-Freudian thinker, applied some prescient psychology in analysing Beatrice's 'natural antipathy' to De Flores as a gaping hole in her own self. One might say now that she seeks completion and that, despite flirtation with Alsemero, only De Flores can provide that final thrilling factor which might even be called love were not class and aesthetics insurmountable obstacles. She's clearly in denial and it's the shared homicide that opens her eyes to her true feelings for her nemesis. Lowell compares Beatrice's 'quivering' (p. 35) desire for a co-committed criminal act with De Flores to Macbeth's terror-seduction by the suspended dagger before him. Both characters experience a 'terrible fascination' that Lowell claims God allows us to cope with by naming it 'the promptings of our evil demon' (p. 35). Rather than deeming Beatrice an innocent creature being preyed upon, Lowell sees her as able to rationalize and lie to herself, 'like a child talking aloud in the dark to relieve its terrors' (p. 36), in order to taste the double forbidden fruits of murder and lust. She is rendered childlike by the 'ravished intercourse between her passions and her affections' and driven into 'the wilderness of bleak loneliness' (p. 36) by her guilt.

Ultimately, Lowell's appreciation for Beatrice is a sympathetic one, seeing her dimensions and complexity in a positive light, unlike William Archer in *The Old Drama and the New* (1923) who savages the play itself as unbelievable and sensationalistic. He slams Middleton (he won't stoop to analyse Rowley's 'distasteful and tedious underplot') for exploiting lust and horror to the detriment of character development. Archer finds no truth or psychology in this play and damns the plot as 'utterly feeble and inexplicable' (p. 96). In his reading Beatrice becomes De Flore's mistress because she has had an argument with Alsemero and wants to make him suffer for it. He finds it preposterous that Beatrice would put her faith and virginity in the hands of a 'hideously ugly and ruffianly retainer' (p. 97). Archer even suggests a better plot twist: that a 'needy adventurer' or a 'moonstruck youth' (p. 97) would be a better dramatic choice if there's cuckolding to be done. For him, Beatrice is over-simplified and over-emotional to the point of bad comedy. He suggests she either stand up to her blackmailer or accept the protection of her fiancé. His next suggestion is equal parts prudish and explicit: that Beatrice takes De Flores as a lover but as a 'moderate one who will not break her hymen before her wedding night' (p. 97). He imagines the 'importunate' De Flores as unable to hold up his part of that bargain.

When all is said and done Archer files Middleton away among the 'minor Elizabethans' (p. 96) and his conservative interpretation shows a mind desperately seeking an alternative reality where *The Changeling* retains the moral centre of John Reynolds' original storyline. It's a Calvinist reading that begs the question: was *The Changeling* ahead of its time or just ambiguous enough to easily stand up to Freudian interpretation? Archer finds it to be a work devoid of morality as if he expects it to be traditional moral parable. Lowell finds more shades of complexity in the characters but is it a sign of his times that for him Beatrice must be 'like a child' (p. 37) in her denial. Is Lowell reading the text as Middleton and Rowley intended or is Archer closer to the mark and the playwrights just botched the moral with improbable storytelling? Archer clearly wants Beatrice to be something she's not, a tougher cookie with better taste in her transgressions. Lowell accepts Beatrice's choices but with the assumption that her love–hate for De Flores motivates her rather than any conventional understanding of right and wrong.

Two great champions of this play, contributing to its continued study during the 'dark nights' of its 300-year hiatus from performance, were the poets A.C. Swinburne and T.S. Eliot. Like his contemporaries, Swinburne in his *The Age of Shakespeare* (1908) casts derision on the 'underplot' that, like many Victorians, he finds 'very stupid, rather coarse, and almost vulgar' (p. 182). What he fails to enjoy in the subplot, Swinburne more than makes up for in his ebullient praise for the main one. Writing in 1886 he proclaimed the character of De Flores to be 'perfect and living'; for him only Shakespeare wrote a role so 'horrible human, so fearfully and wonderfully natural' (p. 182). De Flores' 'passionately cynical desire' (p. 182) is what enchants Swinburne. This tunnel vision drives the servant in a way that reveals an ultimate truth about human nature, 'a touch worthy of the greatest dramatist who ever lived' (p. 184). Beatrice is 'head-strong, unscrupulous' and 'haughty' and Swinburne relishes her fall into De Flores' 'very clutch' (p. 184). For him it's clearly a morality play where her pride goeth before her fall and he gives no credence to the idea that she might have suspected, at least subconsciously, that De Flores would collect his debt in flesh. For Swinburne it's entirely about her hubris coming home to roost, the wages of having 'a nature absolutely incapable of seeing more than one thing or holding more than one thought at a time' (p. 184). As with Lowell, Swinburne's reading, for all its admiration for Middleton and Rowley's artistry, is that Beatrice is ultimately just a girl blind to the effects of her actions. He even sees a 'lurid streak of tragic humor' (p. 185) in her horrifying undoing, an interpretation that summons up the image of the damned hero in a medieval morality play meeting his deserved fate, flailing in a painted 'hell mouth'. The image is backed up by the fact that the double homicide happens in Alsemero's closet, an apt substitute for the classic set piece.

Another great admirer of Middleton and the Jacobeans, T.S. Eliot explained in his essay on Middleton in 1927 that the writer never became better known because his style was too diverse and his collaboration so seamless that one can't put a finger on just who he was. There may always be some doubt as to who Shakespeare really was but most of his plays are clearly worthy of his name. Eliot calls Middleton 'impersonal' (p. 161, *Selected* Essays, 1934, p. 161) and so protean that he might in fact be the eponymous changeling. 'He has no message' (p. 163) and the only thing that's certain for Eliot is that he wrote great plays. He bestows somewhat backhanded praise on all of Middleton as 'long-winded and tiresome but punctuated by sudden reality' (p. 163). Reading Middleton, one gets lulled by what seems to be a morality play, only to get knocked off one's horse by 'a dispassionate exposure of fundamental passions of any time and any place' (p. 163). While Eliot sees *The Changeling*'s basic plot as an absurd, conventional one (one that we still see repeated in the modern thriller or film noir) Eliot still unearths a 'stratum of truth' (p. 164) beneath the dull surface. He compares the play to Ibsen's *A Doll's House*, Sophocles' *Oedipus* and Shakespeare's *Antony and Cleopatra*, where the protagonists are not evil, just 'irresponsible and underdeveloped' (p. 164) and Fortune's fools. His view of Beatrice is that she, like a child, 'is not a moral creature; she becomes moral only by becoming damned' (p. 164). He uses the term 'habituation' (p. 165) to describe the snowball effect of bad things Beatrice racks up once she gets involved with De Flores, like Macbeth once the Witches and his wife have set him in motion. Ultimately Beatrice is a closer partner to De Flores because of their murderous complicity than she could ever be to be her intended, Alsemero, who she no longer thinks about. The point Eliot underlines repeatedly is that tragedies like the one of Beatrice and De Flores 'happen every day and perpetually' (p. 166). Middleton may have no message but his ear as a 'great recorder' (p. 169) is second only to Shakespeare's. While Eliot refutes it as a morality play it is clearly a cautionary tale against living a lie. Like Nora in *A Doll's House* and Oedipus, Beatrice wakes up from her delusion with a warning for our own. Eliot's interpretation might be a bridge between the Moralists and the Freudians.

While most early critics ignore or abuse the comic subplot, William Empson took it seriously and analysed its uses in *Some Views of Pastoral* (1935). He posits that Rowley's madhouse story is shied away from because in it one has to embrace the 'unembarrassed Elizabethan view of lunatics' (p. 48) just as one must face the anti-Semitism of Shakespeare's *Merchant of Venice* in order to delve into that tale. Empson puts forth that Shakespeare's lunatics are more acceptable for their 'surrealist' (p. 49) handling whereas Middleton's are more realistic and therefore more brutal. He contrasts the comparable bird-caged women from the two plots in that Isabella is 'sane; living among madmen' (p. 49) while Beatrice and De Flores are the crazy ones. He plays up the folk-tale element of the changeling as a fairy child exchanged for a human one. Antonio, a faux fool, might just 'snatch her (Isabella) into his world' (p. 50). He dubs De Flores the eponymous changeling, comparing him to the madhouse keeper Lollio and points up the paralleled blackmail plots. Rather than a throwaway storyline as the critics above dismiss, the 'underplot' scenes serve as well-crafted foreshadowing to the tragic events that follow them. He also points out that Alsemero's callous de-virginising of Diaphanta 'is more really brutal than anything in the asylum scenes' (p. 50). This points out the inherent morality in Isabella's decision to cunningly sidestep the advances of the two feigned lunatics and their untrustworthy warden, while Beatrice opens her heart to Alsemero and her body to De Flores. But would Isabella have tasted the forbidden fruit Antonio offers if he had only been a gentleman to her madwoman persona? Again, morality proves a movable feast, even in the more cartoonish of the two plots.

## Moralizing Beatrice

Roberta Barker and David Nicol may have put the play's moral question most succinctly with the title of their 2004 article 'Does Beatrice Have a Subtext?' Setting up the two sides of the aisle on the question of how to analyse Beatrice, the authors contend that either one sees this as a morality play or a 'dark love story about the bond between two well-matched demon lovers' (p.1). They contend that the 'more romantic' (p. 2) of the two options (i.e. demon lovers) is the one favoured by twentieth- and twenty-first-century stage interpretations, fuelled by the reviews of homogeneously Freud-based stage critics. Most literary critics interpret the character of Beatrice as either a naive victim or a Jacobean 'formidable woman' while actresses and directors from the play's 'revival' in 1961 up to the present portray an awakening to 'her slow realization of her repressed, sub-textual desire for De Flores' (p. 2). The critic Una Ellis-Fremor, however, describes Beatrice's journey as that of a 'woman sleep-walking'; only after she has caused a murder is she able to awake to 'that world of reality she has wandered into' (1964, p. 147). Does this let Beatrice off the hook for her crimes or is it an indictment of a society where young women are raised in captivity and therefore morally rootless? Either way it's the shock of having contributing to killing an innocent man that awakens conscience in Beatrice. Why doesn't it work for De Flores? If Beatrice awakes to her reality then it must be a bloody, duplicitous one, based on her subsequent actions that include some manner of submission to adultery and another assisted homicide.

The distance between page and stage is clearly a great one and one wonders if the gap between theory and practice can be bridged. In a work of criticism one can more easily place oneself in a foreign time and place, submerging oneself in what we can discover of the worldview of the Jacobeans. When staged, however, is it ever possible to leave behind our modern sensibilities and go with the flow of an unrepentantly male-dominated society where women and the use of their bodies are commodities to be traded? Can anyone with even a layman's understanding of psychology and sexuality put themselves in the shoes of Middleton and Rowley's Jacobean audience while watching the plight of Beatrice? If, as the writer David Mamet claims, drama is where we go to see characters acting courageously, it becomes vital to choose just what Beatrice is fighting against. It will be a long evening in the theatre if Beatrice is simply a 'bad woman' just as Richard III or Macbeth will bore us if they're just homicidal despots. It's strong if she's bucking the system of Jacobean patriarchy, but only if that society's oppression can be rendered convincingly on stage. If she's at war with *herself*, striving to get what she wants despite the warnings of her conscience and her soul, then her choices must be seen to run counter to one another. She is literally fighting herself but symbolically the figures of Alsemero and De Flores might stand in for her better and worse natures.

I'll come back to Barker and Nicol and Beatrice's performance-based assessment but first let's look at a sample of critics who interpret her motivations based purely on the text. For some Beatrice is easily categorized as a simple, murderous black widow. Gamaliel Bradford found her 'thoroughly hateful' while still holding 'an irresistible fascination' for him ('The Women of Middleton and Webster', 1921, p. 18). Contrasting her passion to that of Juliet, Bradford deems that for her 'caprice is law' and the murder plot comes suddenly 'into her poor, flighty, unmoral brain' (p. 18). T.F. Wharton calls Beatrice a 'moral ignoramus' who submits to De Flores purely for 'punitive satisfaction' since she is indeed 'the deed's creature' (*Moral Experiment in Jacobean Drama*, 1988, p. 135). Bradford, while referring to Beatrice as a 'sweet, foolish devil' tells readers that she 'lacks neither imagination nor intellect, but only heart and conscience' (p. 19). Going on to posit that her 'monstrous pride' is 'the only strong thing in her' (p. 20) Bradford's misogynist reading makes one want to double-check the date of his essay, which feels more 1621 than 1921. His use of phrases like 'it has penetrated even her poor, silly, idle brain' (p. 20) raise alarm bells and stir late-twentieth-century critics like Deborah G. Burks and Sara Eaton, who go after a patriarchal Jacobean society rather than casting blame on a morally depraved Beatrice. The condescension of nineteenth- and early-twentieth-century critics (Lowell aside) creates a backlash of readings in defence of Beatrice's behaviour in the late twentieth century.

In her '"I'll Want My Will Else"; The Changeling and Women's Complicity with Their Rapists' (1995), Burks psychoanalyses the rape laws on the books at the time the play was written. She presents Beatrice and Isabella as victims of the commerce that traded in a 'woman's sexual continence and submission to the authority of their fathers and husbands' (p. 762). Submitting the model of Lucrece, ravished victim of Tarquin, as the period's idealized, pure-but-defiled archetype, Burks contrasts her martyrdom with that of 'De Flores' whore' (p. 763). 'Symptomatic of a pervasive fear of women's desire' (p. 763), Beatrice becomes the misogynist's poster girl for all that is dangerous in woman. The unnatural fact that she dares to enter into a 'contest of wills' (p. 771) with her father leads to the swathe of male victims she leaves in her wake. For Burks every wife at that time was a trophy wife, a piece of cherished property that paranoid males needed to guard from the 'seduction of sexual assault' (p. 763). The economic and political crises of the 1620s heightened this already intense hysteria in men, a time when the word 'rape' meant both 'submission to unwanted sex' as well 'abduction'. Both meant loss of status and property for the 'owner' (which was not legally the woman). For Burks, Middleton and Rowley 'deliberately echo the language of ravishment law' (p. 772) in order to play upon the anxieties of their male audience. She stresses the fundamental connection between 'this family's sexual and social welfare both of which are undermined by Beatrice-Joanna's corruption' (p. 772). The character's deceit and subtlety make her the ultimate nightmare to her society. She seems virtuous but beneath the surface she represents all that men fear: sexual degradation and social bankruptcy. Burks' thesis is that Middleton and Rowley's morality play underscores the logic of laws 'concerned that women might lack the moral sense to conduct themselves appropriately' (p. 782). Beatrice might as well appear in a devil costume, since she represents just that figure (Webster got to the title *The White Devil* a decade earlier but it could apply here if Burks is correct). Burks sees no possibility for a greater awareness on the part of the authors: for them Beatrice's will and desires are 'a diabolic mirroring of Jacobean sexual mores' (p. 776).

This interpretation reads *The Changeling* as a morality play devoid of romance and humanity. Middleton and Rowley's play becomes a piece of propaganda, not for the proselytizing Christianity of John Reynolds, but for their male-dominated Jacobean society where rape is prohibited by law merely because it involves another man's property. Burks uses the social history of the law books to make her case but as to what really went on behind closed doors we can only imagine. While the letter of the law at the time is of interest to some it largely ignores the main characters, Beatrice and De Flores, while explaining the already dubious motivations of more two-dimensional tools like Vermandero, Alibius and the would be 'owner' of Beatrice, Alsemero.

Covering similar territory, Sara Eaton's 'Beatrice-Joanna and the Rhetoric of Love' (1984) presents a heroine trapped in the dual roles of virgin and whore. At once idealized by Alsemero and degraded by De Flores, Beatrice 'becomes an apparently harmonious representation of their conflicting desires' (p. 372). The paradox is the one of 'the fallen Eve' and Middleton certainly lays the Eden garden imagery on with a trowel. Eaton suggests the authors point out Beatrice's contradictions using the 'rhetoric of Courtly Love' (p. 372), i.e. the standard playbook for romantic conduct of the times. She points out the overwhelming amount of asides that undermine characters' court-friendly double-speak; these are private thoughts that illuminate what's really going on. Public talk, what Eaton calls 'the veneer', is for romance while private ones reveal 'physical corruption' (p. 373). She points out that asides almost disappear by Act V, where private thought has become the spoken one.

Eaton sees *The Changeling* as essentially repressive towards women. Peace can only be achieved by Beatrice's 'silencing' and cites her beloved Alsemero's attempt to trap her with the chemicals of his 'closet' and his later imprisonment of her in a literal closet. She outwits the former and is killed before the latter can contain her sexuality, making her a 'woman-as-monster'(p. 374) who shatters Alsemero and Vermandero's hopes for a restored Eden where the rules of Courtly Love trump the sloppy, dark truth of earthly desires. While operating in the same subterranean plane, De Flores' dreams are no less destructive to Beatrice. Thinking only of 'his digestive tract' (p. 376), his desire is to consume her and he constantly uses imagery that entails using her. For Eaton, De Flores and Alsemero's 'projection of desire onto Beatrice-Joanna seem to shape the play's rhetoric' (p. 375). Beatrice buys into the fallacies of Courtly Love as 'She begins to perceive the world around her through male eyes. She becomes the Eve around whom Paradise will collapse' (p. 377). At the same time she personifies the 'Otherness' (p. 379) that the men around her cannot brook. As in Burks, there is no place for a Beatrice in this patriarchy. She cannot be controlled so she must be destroyed. Again, this interpretation sees no empowered agency in Beatrice. She's a victim with no hope of overcoming the stacked deck from which her society is dealing.

Christopher Ricks in 'The Moral and Political Structure of *The Changeling*' (1960) shows morality in Middleton and Rowley in terms of the use of innuendo. While more explicit in the comedic madhouse scenes, the tragic plot nevertheless uses double entendre and insinuation to make strong statements about what lies beneath the surface of the characters' words and actions. Ricks gives an example in Jasperino and Diaphanta's sexual negotiation that follows the first romantic conversation between Alsemero and Beatrice. The latter's 'smooth façade' (p. 292) is unmasked by juxtaposing the former couple's flagrant hook-up. Ricks focuses on words' double-meanings: service (to work for/have sex with), blood (lust/murder), will (lust/self will), act/deed (murder/sex), employment (use/have sex with), performance (deed/sex act) and forward (brave/lustful) which act as markers to 'sum up the moral and poetic theme of the play' (p. 293).

Ricks ties the two plots together through their use of mirrored innuendo and avers that the sub-plot's 'crude buffoonery' (p. 291) make it safe for the main plot to use the same entendres to more subtle effect. De Flores' thrusting of his fingers into Beatrice's discarded glove may be just as graphic as the image of other men inserting 'fingers' into Alibius' wife's 'ring', but the former is delivered with lyricism and brevity compared to the crude violations described in a cavalier manner by Lollio and his employer.

For Ricks, 'Beatrice wants simply to have her cake and eat it, but for that you need two cakes; and what are, at first, two meanings, are inexorably one word' (p. 293). He does not believe that Beatrice uses double meanings knowingly. Ricks is another critic who sees no agency in this heroine, this time using linguistic analysis to make the point rather than social analysis like the authors above. For him Beatrice intends only one meaning for service and deed, having only murder on her mind rather than the appeasement of a forbidden lust, as De Flores does. In her 'Hardness becomes the visage of a man well' (II, ii, 92) entreaty Ricks posits that De Flores doesn't see the murder scheme coming and is only thinking of the sexual meaning of her 'service' and 'employment' (despite the fact that De Flores is an omnipresent watcher and surely sees her newly acquired lust for Alsemero). The scenes between Beatrice and De Flores are liberally peppered with innuendo and Ricks' theory that only De Flores is aware of the double meanings being bandied about is surely one way to play their relationship. The question remains whether what Ricks calls Beatrice's 'tragic incomprehension' (p. 298) raises the stakes at the loss of this anti-heroine's depth. While distancing himself from N.W. Bawcutt's (1958) assertion that Beatrice is a dummy and a lousy judge of character, Ricks posits that she is simply blinded by her own tunnel vision and misses reading De Flores' lustful overtures. While giving a small patch of ground to the idea that Beatrice might be making (pre) Freudian slips by hating De Flores so violently with no good reason, Ricks ultimately espouses reading Beatrice as blind-sided by De Flores' understanding of her own double meanings.

Turning back to Barker and Nicol's 'Does Beatrice Have a Subtext?' one finds a compelling case for what Beatrice is not (i.e. a spoiled child turned awakened sensualist) but not necessarily what she truly is. The authors chart a trend in stage reviewers from 1961 to 1993 that almost exclusively perceives Beatrice as a romantic figure and 'blinkered sex kitten' rather than as a 'formidable woman' (2004, p. 41–42) who falls victim to a rape. Barker and Nicol cite the uniformity of reviewers' dissatisfaction with overall portrayals of Beatrice by Mary Ure (1961), Emma Piper (1978), Diana Quick (1978), Miranda Richardson (1988) and Cheryl Campbell (1993). For the authors the Freudian love–hate interpretation of the De Flores/ Beatrice relationship by early stage reviewers had not changed over a 30-year span but rather become the canonical one. In this view 'no-means-yes' and because Beatrice is a spoiled, rich brat she's in need of a waking up to her forbidden desire for De Flores. Each of the five actresses playing Beatrice have a different obstacle to overcome (class, race, ugliness) but Barker and Nicol see a uniform predilection on the part of directors, actresses and reviewers to a hypocritical, protests-too-much Beatrice aching for a dark-hearted lover.

Drama critics, unable to find the perfect blend of naive child and hard-bitten femme fatale in any of these actors, couch their criticism in terms of the inability of these women to embody a role the reviewers themselves have imagined and idealized. Barker and Nicol use a historicist, feminist theory that modern critics and directors have ignored both Jacobean society and the text itself to rationalize their own oppressive ideas of a virgin/whore Beatrice. Their claim is that the no-means-yes reading by critics and directors is wishful thinking on their part. They demand a whore where there is none. For the authors, critic Irving Wardle's interpretation that Beatrice is 'an enigmatic noblewoman whose power comes from her class as well as from her sexual allure' (quoted in Barker and Nicol, 2004, p. 8) is a more compelling choice than the trend of sheltered-girl-turned-femme-fatale that objectifies London's twentieth-century stage Beatrices. They see the enjoyed-rape fantasy of reviewers as a product of Freud and Stanislavsky, making a fetish of an imagined subtext that distorts the play's true message. But while building an argument that seeking an idealized virgin-whore in the role is not only sleazy but historically unsubstantiated, the authors give short shrift to just who Beatrice might really be. For Barker and Nicol the idea that this play is a love story is based on specious, poor reading of the text. The authors return to an almost nineteenth-century morality, but this time a pro-Beatrice one, where she unquestionably loves only Alsemero (a role marginalized by reviewers) and in reality has no subtext. The proof is in her ongoing devotion to Alsemero, her silence during her rape, and subsequent ruing of ever getting involved with De Flores. Her tragedy is (as with Eaton and Burks above) her failure to tow the line set by male authority and she falls 'more from her desperation to maintain a semblance of obedience to the patriarchal code than from a fulfilment of any hidden desire' (p. 35). For Barker and Nicol, Beatrice doesn't have to wake up to her true nature; the real self was always there in plain sight. When she 'pursues her own will without considering the consequences' (p. 41) the morality play kicks in full force but it's her own initiative that drives her, not a subconscious force that brings out the whore in the virgin.

The question remains whether critical interpretation of *The Changeling* on paper can ever truly sync up with what's shown on stage. Is a Beatrice who is un-tempted by De Flores and just an unfortunate rape victim as stimulating to a twenty-first-century audience as the demon lover who finds her perfect dark match in seemingly her greatest enemy? Would one rather see a play about the historical brutality of the Jacobean patriarchy or a woman who, fighting the system, goes down in a blaze of bloody glory? Assuming that Middleton and Rowley did, as Eliot posits, write without an agenda it would then be open to the interpreter to constantly reinvent the play. This means that the actor, the director and the critic would be correct in their choices as long as the viewer or reader discerns the ring of truth in their interpretation. If Mary Ure's Beatrice struck reviewers as too mannered and tame to embody the collection of opposing forces at work in the role then it makes no difference if historically women were traded like livestock. The audience may want to see her lash out with her sexuality and violence. They may be fickle and want her punished afterwards or they might see her love suicide as her ultimate triumph. The live audience is there for *catharsis*, not historicity. They want the characters to go where they don't dare to go, to heights of emotion that would kill them (or at least ruin their comfortable lives). A work of criticism can afford to demand that the characters be more buttoned down, that they represent the norm of their times, that they ultimately make quantifiable sense. This is the gap between the page and the stage, a tension impossible to reconcile because the demands are so opposed.

# Further Reading

Almost every book ever written about theatre during Jacobean times makes some mention of *The Changeling* and its place as one of the great plays of the era. I was by no means exhaustive in my selections of texts but benefited greatly from the online resources MUSE and JSTOR which most often pointed me in the right direction. The Taylor and Lavagnino *Collected Works* is a good place to start if you're looking for encyclopaedic information on the play and the period and below are the readings I found useful in further understanding this fascinating work.

## Texts and early performances

Bell, Maureen (2007) 'Booksellers Without an Author 1627–1685' in *Thomas Middleton and Early Textual Modern Culture,* Oxford: Clarendon Press. On how plays were sold in Jacobean times.

Neill, Michael (ed.) (2006) *The Changeling*. By Thomas Middleton and William Rowley, New Mermaids, London: A & C Black. Features a strong introduction, especially useful for dates and sources.

Taylor, Gary and John Lavagnino (eds) (2007) *Thomas Middleton: The Collected Works* and *Thomas Middleton and Early Modern Textual Culture*, Oxford: Clarendon Press.

Williams, George Walton (ed.) (1966) *The Changeling*. By Thomas Middleton and William Rowley, Regents Renaissance, Lincoln/London: University of Nebraska Press. Another introduction featuring a clear telling of the play's history.

## Intellectual and cultural context

Bamford, Karen (2000) *Sexual Violence on the Jacobean Stage*, New York: St. Martin's Press.

Bromham, A. A. and Zara Bruzzi (1990) *The Changeling and the Years of Crisis, 1619–1624*, London/New York: Pinter. A debatable hypothesis that *The*

*Changeling* is a work of political protest, this book was most useful in its portrayal of the troubled times.

Brooke, Nicholas (1979) *Horrid Laughter in Jacobean Tragedy*, London: Open Books. On the psychology of gruesomeness and the ties between the tragic and comedic plots.

Ford, John (1970) *Three Plays*, London: Penguin. Specifically his *'Tis Pity She's a Whore*.

Miller, John (2006) *The Stuarts*, London/New York: Hambledon Continuum. For a detailed account of unstable political conditions under James I.

Middleton, Thomas (1968) *Women Beware Women*, London: Ernest Benn,

Ornstein, Robert (1960) *The Moral Vision of Tragedy*, Madison: University of Wisconsin Press. For a defence of the subplot.

Porter, Roy (ed.) (1991) *The Faber Book of Madness*, London: Faber & Faber. Eyewitness accounts of asylum conditions in the seventeenth century.

Pritchard, R. E. (ed.) (1999) *Shakespeare's England*, London: Sutton.

Reed Jr, Robert Rentoul (1970) *Bedlam on the Jacobean Stage*, New York: Octagon Books.

Webster, John (1972) *Three Plays*, London: Penguin. Specifically his *The White Devil* and *The Duchess of Malfi*.

Wilson, A. N. (2006) *London: A History*, New York: Modern Library. A brief but vivid lay of the land.

## Sources: Middleton

Cespedes y Meneses, Gonzalo de (1653) *Gerardo, the unfortunate Spaniard, : or a pattern for lascivious lovers. Containing several strange miseries of loose affections*, S.l. Printed by William Bentley and are to be sold by William Shears at the Bible in S. Pauls Church-yard, I read an internet resource version through the Duke University library system.

Reynolds, John (1997) *The Triumph of God's Revenge against the Crying and Excrable Sinne of Wilful and Premeditated Murder*, Cambridge: Chadwyck-Healey. Resource: Literature Online.

## Sources: Rowley

Redd Jr, Robert Rentoul (1970) *Bedlam on the Jacobean Stage*, New York: Octagon Books.

# Key performances and productions

## Theatre for a New Audience

Interview:

Director Robert Woodruff, telephone interview with the author, August 2010.

Reviews:

Marks, Peter (1997) 'The Changeling', *New York Times*, 8 March: http://theater.nytimes.com/mem/theater/treview.html?pagewanted=print&res=9b05e2d71130f93ba35750c0a961958260.

Sommer, Elyse (1997) 'The Changeling', *CurtainUp*: www.curtainup.com/changel.html

## Quantum Theatre

www.quantumtheatre.com

Interview:

Director Dan Jemmett, telephone interview with the author, July 2010.

Rawson, Christopher (2005) 'Tale of Lust and Revenge Takes a Quantum Leap from Paris to Pittsburgh', *Pittsburgh Post-Gazette*, 11 March: www.post-gazette.com/pg/05070/469375-42.stm

Preview/Review:

Rawson, Christopher (2005) 'New "Dog", Old Source', *Pittsburgh Post-Gazette*, 11 March: www.post-gazette.com/pg/05070/469376-42.stm

Rawson, Christopher (2005) 'Quantum's "Dogface" a Raw Tale of Sexy Beasts', *Pittsburgh Post-Gazette*, 16 March: www.post-gazette.com/pg/05075/471898-42.stm

## Cheek By Jowl

www.cheekbyjowl.com

Interviews:

Website podcasts (www.cheekbyjowl.com/the_changeling.php):

'Olivia Williams, Tom Hiddleston and Will Keen Talk about Their Roles in *The Changeling*', 31 July 2006.

'Interview with Olivia Williams', 8 March 2006.

'Interview with Tom Hiddleston and Will Keen', 8 March 2006.

'Interview with Declan Donnellan', 9 March 2006.

Reviews:

Alfree, Claire (2006) *Metro*:
www.metro.co.uk/metrolife/13509-metrolife-the-changeling

Billington, Michael (2006) *Guardian*, 16 May:
www.guardian.co.uk/stage/2006/may/16/theatre

Cavendish, Dominic (2006) *Telegraph*, 8 May:

www.telegraph.co.uk/culture/theatre/3652215/From-kitchen-table-to-global-stage.html

Clapp, Susannah (2006) *Observer*, 21 May:
www.guardian.co.uk/stage/2006/may/21/theatre

Peter, John (2006) *Sunday Times*, 21 May:
www.cheekbyjowl.com/the_changeling.php

## English Touring Theatre

www.ett.org

Reviews:

Ashworth, Pat (2007) *Stage*, 8 October:
www.thestage.co.uk/reviews/review.php/18445/the-changeling

Coombe, Geoffrey, 'Your Reviews':
www.ett.org.uk/productions/50/the-changeling

Hickling, Alfred (2007) *Guardian*, 4 October:
www.guardian.co.uk/stage/2007/oct/04/theatre1

Morley-Priestman, Ann (2007) *whatsonstage.com*, 17 October:
www.whatsonstage.com/index.php?pg=207&story=E8821192627808&title=The+Changeling+(tour)

Orme, Steve (2007) *British* Theatre Guide:
www.britishtheatreguide.info/reviews/ETTchangeling-rev.htm

## Caffeine Theatre's *The Changeling* and *Tallgrass Gothic*

www.caffeinetheatre.com

Interviews:

*Tallgrass Gothic* director Jennifer Shook and dramaturg Dan Smith, interview with the author, June 2010.
Actor Jeremy van Meter, e-mail interview with the author, July 2010.
Actor Amanda Powell, e-mail interview with the author, July 2011.

Reviews:

Barnidge, Mary Shen (2009) *Windy City Times*, 25 March: http://windycitymediagroup.com/gay/lesbian/news/ARTICLE.php?AID=20767
Beer, John (2009) *Time Out Chicago*, 25 March:
http://timeoutchicago.com/arts-culture/theater/62638/the-changelingtallgrass-gothic

## The play on screen

### BBC 1974

*Helen Mirren at the BBC* (BBC Worldwide, 19 February 2008). DVD extras include interview with Helen Mirren (Beatrice).

### BBC 1993

*Performance: The Changeling* (DVD, directed by Simon Curtis, starring Bob Hoskins, Elizabeth McGovern, Hugh Grant, Leslie Phillips).

### Middleton's Changeling

www.marcusthompson.com. Great back-story on the trials and tribulations of making a low budget film of the play.

## Critical assessments

### Collections

Holdsworth, R. V. (ed.) (1990) *Three Jacobean Restoration Tragedies* (Basingstoke: Macmillan). A source for a host of often contrasting essays on the play.

### Specific works cited in this chapter

Archer, William (1923) *The Old and the New*, pp. 96–100, extracted from Holdsworth. A puritan rant against the infeasibility of the plot.

Barker, Roberta and David Nicol (2004) 'Does Beatrice Have a Subtext?: *The Changeling* on the London Stage' *Early Modern Literary Studies* 10: 1, 31–43. Invaluable to understanding the entire span of not only dramatic criticism but onstage interpretation of the role.

Bawcutt, N. W. (1958) 'The Double Plot of *The Changeling*', The Revels Plays, Manchester: Manchester University Press.

Bradford, Gamaliel (1921) 'The Women of Middleton and Webster', *Sewanee Review* 29: 1, 14–29, reprinted on JSTOR by Johns Hopkins University Press. Beatrice as naive brat.

Burks, Deborah (1995) ' "I'll Want My Will Else": The Changeling and Women's Consent with Their Rapists', *ELH* 62: 4, 759–90. An argument against Beatrice as a strong woman acting on her own agency.

Eaton, Sara (1984) 'Beatrice-Joanna and the Rhetoric of Love in *The Changeling*', *Theatre Journal* 36: 3, 371–8. The misogyny of courtly romantic language.

Eliot, T. S. (1934) 'Thomas Middleton', *Selected Essays*, 161–9. Extracted from Holdsworth, Middleton as a writer without a moral agenda.

Ellis-Fermor, Una (1964) *The Jacobean Drama: An Interpretation*, New York: Vintage. Beatrice as sleep-walker.

Empson, William (1935) *Some Versions of Pastoral*, extracted from Holdsworth. An early, sympathetic view of the madhouse plot.

Lowell, James Russell (1843) 'The Plays of Thomas Middleton', *The Pioneer*, vol. 1 (January). A very rare pre-Freudian read of Beatrice's motivations.

Randall, Dale B. J. (1984) 'Some Observations on the Theme of Chastity in *The Changeling*', *English Literary Renaissance* 14, 347–66.

Ricks, Christopher (1960) 'The Poetic and Moral Structure of *The Changeling*', *Essays in Criticism* X , 290–306. Beatrice as clueless to her own linguistic double-meaning.

Swinburne, Algernon Charles (1908) *The Age of Shakespeare*, New York/ London: Harper & Brothers. The blindness of an innocent Beatrice.

Wharton, T. F. (1988) *Moral Experiment in Jacobean Drama*, London: Macmillan. Beatrice as guilty idiot.

# Index